D0083090

Care, Autonomy, and Justice

FEMINIST THEORY AND POLITICS

Virginia Held and Alison Jaggar, Series Editors

Care, Autonomy, and Justice: Feminism and the Ethic of Care,
Grace Clement

A Mind of One's Own: Feminist Essays on Reason and Objectivity,
edited by Louise M. Antony and Charlotte Witt

Sexual Democracy: Women, Oppression, and Revolution,
Ann Ferguson

Gender, Identity, and the Production of Meaning,
Tamsin E. Lorraine

Rocking the Ship of State: Toward a Feminist Peace Politics,
edited by Adrienne Harris and Ynestra King

Reproducing the World: Essays in Feminist Theory,
Mary O'Brien

Care, Autonomy, and Justice
Feminism and the Ethic of Care

Grace Clement

WestviewPress
A Division of HarperCollins*Publishers*

For my parents,
Bea and Blanton Clement,
and my son, Benjamin

Feminist Theory and Politics

Copyright © 1996 by Westview Press, A Division of HarperCollins Publishers, Inc.

Published in 1996 in the United States of America by Westview Press, 5500 Central Avenue, Boulder, Colorado 80301-2877, and in the United Kingdom by Westview Press, 12 Hid's Copse Road, Cumnor Hill, Oxford OX2 9JJ

Library of Congress Cataloging-in-Publication Data
Clement, Grace.
    Care, autonomy, and justice : feminism and the ethic of care / by Grace Clement.
       p. cm. — (Feminist theory and politics)
    Includes bibliographical references and index.
    ISBN 0-8133-2537-4. —— ISBN 0-8133-2538-2. (pbk.)
       1. Caring. 2. Autonomy (Philosophy) 3. Justice (Philosophy) 4. Feminist ethics. I. Title.
II. Series.
BJ1475.C57 1996
177'.7—dc20
                                                    96-8449
                                                  CIP

The paper used in this publication meets the requirements of the American National Standard for Permanence of Paper for Printed Library Materials Z39.48-1984.

10   9   8   7   6   5   4   3   2   1

Contents

▼

▼

Acknowledgments

This book began as a dissertation at Northwestern University. There I received indispensable and generous guidance and support from Nancy Fraser, my dissertation advisor. I am also grateful to Tom McCarthy and Jane Mansbridge, who carefully read my work and offered valuable suggestions for improving it. My fellow students, Andy Norman, Todd Grantham, and Pablo DeGreiff, listened to my ideas and helped me formulate many of the arguments I make.

I finished this project after I began teaching at Salisbury State University, where my colleagues Jim Hatley, Francis Kane, and Jerry Miller have provided a wonderfully supportive work environment, including organizing two departmental functions to discuss my ideas. I have also benefited from an anonymous reader who read an earlier draft of the manuscript and made generous suggestions that helped me improve it. Above all, I am indebted to my husband, Michel Bazin, who has helped me think through my ideas and has provided much-needed support and encouragement throughout this project.

Grace Clement

Introduction

▼

Since the early 1980s, moral philosophers and social scientists, both feminist and non-feminist, have debated the basis, the normative merits, and the implications of the approach to morality called the ethic of care. The ethic of care emphasizes aspects of moral reasoning that are not generally emphasized by dominant Western moral theories, especially by Kantian ethics. Because these aspects of moral reasoning have been most important in women's traditional activities and experiences, the ethic of care has been of special interest to feminist ethicists. In this work I give an overview of the debate between the ethic of care and the predominant ethic of justice, defend a particular point of view on this debate, and show how this debate and the ethic of care are important for moral and feminist theory. In particular, I argue that the ethic of care is an often neglected but essential dimension of ethics, but that we must make distinctions between versions of the ethic based on their roles in challenging or contributing to women's oppression. Doing so requires that we challenge standard accounts of the relationship between care and justice.

The ethic of care and the ethic of justice are especially worthy of our attention because they are not merely two among many different approaches to ethics. They are more fundamental than other possible ethics because they thematize two basic dimensions of human relationships, dimensions that might be called vertical and horizontal. The ethic of justice focuses on questions of equality and inequality, while the ethic of care focuses on questions of attachment and detachment, and both sets of questions can arise in any context. As Carol Gilligan writes:

> All human relationships, public and private, can be characterized *both* in terms of equality and in terms of attachment, and . . . both inequality and detachment constitute grounds for moral concern. Since everyone is vulnerable both to oppression and to abandonment, two moral visions—one of justice and one of care—recur in human experience. The moral injunctions, not to act unfairly toward others, and not to turn away from someone in need, capture these different concerns (Gilligan 1987, 20).

▼

Traditionally, these two ethics have been kept separate from one another, such that each ethic has focused on one dimension of human relationships to the exclusion of the other. This has resulted in extreme forms of the two ethics, in uncaring forms of justice and unjust forms of care. The fact that these ethics have been gender-coded, reflecting and contributing to relations of dominance and subordination, might lead us to think that they are merely symptoms of these particular social conditions. However, these ethics are not merely reflections of gender, but of fundamental dimensions of human relationships, and thus their relationship to one another is of great importance for morality in general, as well as for questions of gender.

My approach differs from three approaches to the care/justice debate frequently taken: the celebration of the ethic of care as a feminine ethic, the assimilation of the ethic of care to a justice perspective, and the rejection of the ethic of care from a feminist perspective. Proponents of the "feminine" approach have as a general goal the recognition and celebration of women's distinctive activities and experiences. They regard the ethic of care as a creation of women which is usually ignored or devalued by male-defined moral theory. While advocates of this feminine approach do not necessarily believe that all or only women use this ethic, their interest in the ethic arises because (they believe) women especially use it. For instance, Carol Gilligan's work is based on psychological research which she believes demonstrates women's particular use of the ethic of care. Others, like Nel Noddings and Sara Ruddick, do not rely on empirical research, but explore the ethic implicit in and arising out of traditionally female practices like child-rearing.

This feminine approach examines the implications of women's distinctive approach to morality by moving the ethic of care from the periphery to the center of moral theory. Doing so is thought to reveal that the prevailing ethic of justice and its emphasis on autonomy are often dangerous and illusory. The individualism of standard male-defined approaches to morality is replaced by an emphasis on interdependence and the maintenance of relationships. This approach also challenges the traditional understanding of relations between relative strangers in the male-associated public realm as morally paradigmatic, instead focusing on relations between family members and friends in the female-associated personal realm. The abstract universalism of the ethic of justice is replaced by the contextualism of the ethic of care. In short, traditional approaches to ethics tend to dismiss women's distinctive moral orientation. This feminine approach concludes that it is important to give the ethic of care the credit it deserves, in part by showing how it reveals shortcomings in the prevailing ethic of justice.

An obvious question raised by the above approach is: Is the ethic of care really a women's ethic? If we are asked to celebrate the ethic of care because women use this ethic, then we should first be sure that women really use it. A number of critics have argued that no empirical correlation between women and the ethic of care has been demonstrated. They suggest instead that Gilligan and her collabo-rators "heard" what confirmed the stereotypes of women that they already accepted. Moreover, insofar as Gilligan's "different voice" truly *reflects* anyone's moral orientation, critics argue that it is biased toward the values of the Western, white, well-educated women Gilligan's research has focused on.[1] Similarly, in Noddings's and Ruddick's work, mothers seem to represent all women. Barbara Houston writes:

> The feminist standpoint adopted by Gilligan, Ruddick and Noddings . . . appears to assume a form of female essentialism. That is, despite disclaimers by each of them about the dangers of speaking for all women, there does appear to be the assump-tion that women's experience is similar enough for us to posit a women's ethics aris-ing out of women's distinctive labor. (Houston 1987, 259)

Thus it seems that Gilligan and other advocates of a feminine ethic of care are guilty of the same error Lawrence Kohlberg committed, that of false universalism. While Kohlberg posited the moral experiences of men as *human* moral experience, those defending the ethic of care as a feminine ethic seem to posit the experiences of a specific, nonrepresentative group of women as *women's* moral experience.

This charge of false universalism has linked the debates surrounding the ethic of care to recent feminist debates about the importance of recognizing the differ-ences between women, and about whether despite their differences in race, class, culture, etc., all women share what Marilyn Frye calls "a ghetto of sorts" (Frye 1983, 9). Here, however, I will avoid these debates. I will not be concerned with social-scientific questions about whether women use the ethic of care, and I will not defend the ethic of care on the grounds that women use it. Instead I will focus on questions about the adequacy of the ethic of care as a moral theory. I will ask whether the ethic of care is a satisfactory approach to morality, regardless of who uses it. This does not mean that gender is irrelevant to my study of the ethic of care. Even if many women do not use the ethic of care, this ethic undeniably cap-tures a widely-held view of what women are and ought to be. The ethic of care is socially coded as a *feminine* ethic, while the ethic of justice is socially coded as a *masculine* ethic. We need not make any false generalizations about women to rec-ognize that women's traditional activities and experiences are especially relevant to a study of the ethic of care.

This brings me to the second general approach to the ethic of care that I dis-cuss: The assimilation of the ethic of care to a justice perspective (e.g. Hill 1987, Sher 1987). Moral philosophers who take this approach emphasize the distinction between gender and ethics. They point out that while most histori-cal philosophers have had deplorable things to say about women, this sexism can and should be distinguished from what they have had to say about moral-ity. By restricting our attention to moral questions, they argue, it becomes clear that the debates between "the ethic of care" and "the ethic of justice" are merely contemporary versions of familiar moral debates, such as the Kant/Hume debate over the roles of reason and sentiment in morality. Moreover, even if most moral philosophers have had little to say about care issues, their moral theories generally allow for the ethic of care. Even an ethic of justice, like Kant's, which does not focus on care themes can nevertheless encompass them. In fact, a moral theory can be evaluated by the extent to which it can accommodate the ethic of care and/or the moral views of women. As Susan Moller Okin writes:

> The best theorizing about justice has integral to it the notions of care and empathy. . . . The best theorizing about justice is not good enough if it does not, or cannot readily be adapted to, include women and their points of view as fully as men and their points of view. (Okin 1989, 15)

According to this approach, those who champion the ethic of care tend to caricature the theories they label ethics of justice, assuming, for instance, that universal principles preclude rather than require a close attention to context. Rather than shifting our focus to a new approach, then, we need to examine ethics of justice more carefully to see whether and how they can accommodate care concerns. According to Kant's moral theory, for instance, autonomy is a fundamental value, but it need not be understood individualistically, or threaten our sense of community. Justice and care should not be understood as alternative approaches to morality, but rather as complementary approaches. This approach argues that justice is the proper ethic for our public interactions, while care is the proper ethic for our interactions with family and friends. In short, according to this "justice" approach, the ethic of care need not be rejected, but neither is it an important development in moral theory. Not only have care themes been emphasized in various historical moral theories, such as those of Aristotle and Hume, but the ethic of care can be assimilated by so-called ethics of justice, such as Kant's moral philosophy.

First, I will briefly respond to the charge that the ethic of care is not significantly different from Aristotelian or Humean ethics. Supporting this charge is the fact that the recent interest in the ethic of care has coincided with a renewed interest in virtue ethics. The fundamental difference between the recent attention to the ethic of care and these other traditions is that study of the ethic of care, at least at its best, has brought critical attention to the gender-coding of our moral concepts. It has clarified and challenged the sexual division of moral labor. Aristotle and Hume also made reference to the gender-coding of moral concepts, but they sought to reinforce rather than challenge the sexual division of moral labor. Contemporary ethicists studying virtue ethics do not do this, but they have for the most part ignored gender issues. At least insofar as the ethic of care has been studied from a feminist perspective, it is a significant departure from Aristotelian, Humean, and contemporary virtue ethics.

The relationship between the ethic of care and the ethic of justice depends on one's characterizations of the two approaches. Some versions of the ethic of care

are clearly incompatible with almost any version of the ethic of justice, while other versions of the ethic of care seem compatible with a standard version of the ethic of justice in one way or another. Depending on the precise nature of the two ethics, this complementarity might mean merely that the ethics have distinct spheres of application, or it might mean that the two ethics can be combined into one comprehensive ethic. In this book, I will begin with versions of the ethic of care and the ethic of justice that I will call ideal types. I will focus on three features of the two ethics which are typically emphasized and which serve to define the ethics in opposition to one another. These are the ethics' relative abstractness or concreteness, their priorities, and their conceptions of the self. In particular, I will develop a definition of the ethic of care based on its contextual decisionmaking, its priority of maintaining relationships, and its social conception of the self. In contrast, I will define the ethic of justice in terms of its abstract decision making, its priority of equality, and its individualistic conception of the self. Although I have chosen features that are typical in and which I believe capture the essence of each ethic, my definitions are archetypes that no thinker necessarily holds in the precise forms I have presented. While I will work with versions of the two ethics that are defined in clear opposition to one another, I show that these versions of the ethics are not morally ideal. Instead I will show how the interactions between the ethics can help us sort out better and worse versions of each ethic.

Although I believe that the ethic of justice and the ethic of care are in many ways compatible, I challenge the attempt to assimilate the ethic of care into the ethic of justice. Doing so does not give the ethic of care equal status to the ethic of justice. Instead, it maintains the traditional hierarchy according to which that which is coded as masculine is regarded as more important than that which is coded as feminine. Assimilating care into the ethic of justice *cannot* be done in a way that gives care equal status to justice. It can only be done by interpreting care through the perspective of justice, thereby devaluing and marginalizing it. By maintaining the standard focal points of the ethic of justice, we lose the benefits offered by the focal points of the ethic of care and by the interaction between the ethics' different focal points. Even though the ethic of justice's emphasis on general principles does not preclude attention to context, it creates the impression that general principles are both distinct from and more important than contextual detail. Likewise, while the ethic of justice's individualism does not logically imply that social connections are unimportant, it does have that nonlogical implication (Calhoun 1988, 452).

Thus the care perspective is the central focus of this book. I do not claim that all moral theorists should treat the ethic of care as central. My purpose is to assess the moral value of the ethic of care, and doing so requires that I consider the ethic on its own terms, rather than from the perspective of another approach. While I will work toward integrating the two ethics into a complete account of moral reasoning, I will also remain aware of the real danger that the ethic of care might be assimilated and thus devalued by the ethic of justice.

This brings me to the approach to the ethic of care often taken by feminists. While they acknowledge that the ethic of care is a good ethic in the sense that the world would be a better place if everyone used it, feminists often insist that the important questions do not concern the ethic's intrinsic value, but its social context. In fact, they argue, the ethic of care amounts to a resuscitation of traditional stereotypes of women, stereotypes which are used to rationalize the subordination of women. Joan Williams writes:

> Gender stereotypes were designed to marginalize women. These stereotypes no doubt articulated some values shunted aside by Western culture. But the circumstances of their birth mean they presented a challenge to predominant Western values that was designed to fail, and to marginalize women in the process. (Williams 1991, 97)

According to these critics, the ethic of care is less a creation of women than an unjust demand upon women, as it requires women to take care of men and men's interests at the expense of themselves and their own interests. In other words, the ethic of care compromises the autonomy of the caregiver, and is therefore inconsistent with feminist goals. Moreover, the ethic's restriction to personal contexts means that it is unable to address any large-scale social issues, and thus provides no political resources for challenging women's oppression. In short, according to this approach, the ethic of care is inseparable from women's oppression, and while its celebration may make women feel better about their assigned roles, it still reinforces their subordinate status. As Katha Pollitt writes, "It's a rationale for the status quo, which is why men like it, and a burst of grateful applause, which is why women like it. Men keep the power, but since power is bad, so much the worse for them" (Pollitt 1992, 804).

I think it is important to draw attention to the social context of the ethic of care. But just as it is a mistake to ignore care's social context, it is also a mistake to *reduce* the ethic of care to the distorted ways it is often practiced. We can look for the moral and political possibilities implicit in the ethic of care while actively addressing its dangers. Like those taking the above approach, one of my guiding questions will be: Is the ethic of care helpful or harmful to women? But rather than simply accepting or rejecting the ethic of care, I distinguish between better and worse versions of it. This general approach is not unique to me. Others have asserted that a feminist ethic of care is possible. About the "relational turn" of which the recent interest in the ethic of care is a part, Martha Minow writes:

> Unlike relational thought uninformed by feminist perspectives, feminist work tends to focus also on conflict, power, domination, and oppression as features of relationships. The relational turn thus represents not a denial of or lack of interest in conflict and disunity but a focus on the interpersonal and social contexts in which these and all other human relations occur. (Minow 1991, 198)

Others have also identified necessary conditions for a feminist ethic of care. For instance, Barbara Houston asserts that "If anything is to be declared good, right, or just, it had better be demonstrably good, right, or just for women" (Houston 1987, 261).

My approach expands on such suggestions by focusing on two particular features of the ethic of care. These features are ones which feminists cite as problematic *and* which advocates of the ethic of care consider essential. Because of this conflict, these features serve as fundamental dilemmas for any attempt to develop a feminist ethic of care. The first contested feature is autonomy. As I noted above, feminine advocates of the ethic of care argue that autonomy is an individualistic value that the ethic of care rejects in favor of relational virtues. However, its feminist critics argue that because the ethic of care compromises a caregiver's autonomy, it fails by feminist standards. The second contested feature is the ethic of care's status as a personal ethic, appropriate for our relations with family, friends, or those otherwise close to us, such as students. Again, for its feminine advocates, the ethic's scope gives personal relations the moral attention they deserve, correcting the ethic of justice's view of personal relations as morally insignificant in comparison to public relations. Conversely, its critics argue that a feminist ethic must not be limited to personal relations, and must include a concern for social justice.

I argue that the ethic of care reveals important problems with the concept of autonomy, but that these problems are not present in all versions of autonomy. Likewise, critics are correct to insist on the importance of autonomy, but not all versions of the ethic of care conflict with autonomy. I also argue that advocates of the ethic of care are correct to emphasize the moral centrality of personal relations, but that expanding the boundaries of the ethic of care does not amount to trivializing personal relations. Indeed, it does just the opposite, taking the norms of personal relations as a paradigm for all moral relations. I agree with feminist critics that the ethic of care's personal scope is inadequate, but I argue that the ethic can be expanded beyond this scope in a way that enriches rather than threatens the ethic of justice. In general, then, I argue that the conflicts between care and justice orientations need not lead us to accept one at the expense of the other; indeed, these conflicts can help us distinguish between better and worse versions of each ethic. Most importantly, they allow us to construct a genuinely feminist ethic of care.

Finally, I will briefly outline the book. In Chapter 1, I describe the ideal types of the ethic of care and the ethic of justice in terms of their contextuality, distinctive priorities, and conceptions of the self. That is, I begin by treating care and justice as modes of moral reasoning rather than as modes of practice. Of course, properly understood, morality is a matter of practice as well as of theory, and I will go on in later chapters to focus on aspects of moral practice at issue in discussions of care and justice. In the first chapter, however, I will show how the contrasts between the ideal types of justice and care reasoning give rise to further standard contrasts, according to which the ethic of justice prioritizes autonomy while the ethic of care rejects autonomy as a moral ideal, and according to which the ethic of justice applies to the public sphere and the ethic of care applies to the private sphere.

In the following two chapters, I examine the relationship between care and autonomy and make the argument that a feminist ethic of care must allow for its adherents' autonomy. I begin Chapter 2 by developing an account of autonomy as a moral competence that has both personal and social dimensions. I show that the commonly held view that care and autonomy are mutually exclusive arises because of the excessively individualistic and excessively social conceptions of the self that accompany the ideal types of justice and care. In fact, I show that care and autonomy are not mutually exclusive, but are in many ways interdependent.

Despite their theoretical compatibility, care and autonomy do conflict in practice, and I devote Chapter 3 to exploring the symbolic and institutional structures that construct care and autonomy in opposition to each other in our society. I trace the practical conflicts between care and autonomy to the broader symbolic system that dichotomizes public and private, masculinity and femininity, work and love, and instrumentality and expressivity. I go on to examine two forms of care work, housework and nursing, and show the institutional obstacles to care workers' autonomy. Finally, I suggest that overcoming these obstacles will require challenging the public/private boundaries of the ethic of justice and the ethic of care.

In the following two chapters, I examine the standard public/private boundaries between the ethic of care and the ethic of justice, and I argue that a feminist ethic of care must not be confined to the sphere of personal relations. In Chapter 4, I challenge the dichotomy between public and private spheres, and I show that the ethic of care has moral implications beyond the sphere of personal relations. I also show that the standard distinctions between the two ethics used to support the conventional boundaries are often exaggerated and/or misinterpreted.

In Chapter 5 I explore some of the moral issues that arise in attempts to apply the ethic of care in public contexts. One issue concerns what counts as a public ethic of care. One common suggestion is pacifism. I distinguish between versions of pacifism which reflect the conventional level of the ethic of care and which reflect the highest level of the ethic of care. I also examine debates surrounding the public funding of elder-care. I challenge critics of the welfare state who argue that such public versions of the ethic of care weaken the private ethic of care. In fact, I argue, such programs support healthy family values.

Finally, in Chapter 6, I discuss the significance of the ethic of care and of the care/justice debate for moral philosophy more generally. I show that a feminist ethic of care depends upon its interaction with the ethic of justice and the result-ing departure from its ideal type. I examine several accounts of the relationships between care and justice, and argue that the ethic of justice and the ethic of care are distinct and interdependent ethics which must be integrated in a complete account of moral reasoning.

Notes

1. Patricia Hill Collins does, however, refer to care as Afrocentric (Collins 1990, 215–17).

1

The Ideal Types of Care and Justice

▼

The recent and ongoing care/justice debate has focused on questions about the relationship between predominant approaches to ethics, especially Kantian ethics, labeled the ethic of justice, and the newly articulated ethic of care. The answers to these questions have depended on what I will call the ideal types of the ethic of care and the ethic of justice. These ideal types are rarely defended in the extreme forms I present. My purpose is not to claim that any individual has defended these accounts of care or justice but to clarify the ideal types that underlie and motivate much of the recent discussion of care and justice. In the rest of the book I examine and challenge both these assumptions and the resulting conclusions. Although I maintain that justice and care are different ethics, I also show that they are not always different in the ways indicated by their ideal types.

The most important feature of the ideal types of care and justice is that the two ethics are defined as alternatives to one another. They are understood as conflicting ethics, each with its own ontology, method, and priorities, committed to mutually exclusive values and best suited to different kinds of situations. The two ethics are generally distinguished in three ways: (1) the ethic of justice takes an abstract approach, while the ethic of care takes a contextual approach; (2) the ethic of justice begins with an assumption of human separateness, while the ethic of care begins with an assumption of human connectedness; and (3) the ethic of justice has some form of equality as a priority, while the ethic of care has the maintenance of relationships as a priority. These features in turn are generally taken to result in conflicting evaluations of autonomy and a division of labor between the two ethics along public/private lines.

I will illustrate these standard differences between the ethic of justice and the ethic of care by referring to the Heinz dilemma:

In Europe, a woman was near death from cancer. One drug might save her, a rare form of radium that a druggist in the same town had discovered. The druggist was charging $2000, ten times what the drug cost him to make. The sick woman's husband, Heinz, went to everyone he knew to borrow the money, but he could only

11

▼

get together about half of what it cost. He told the druggist that his wife was dying, and asked him to sell it cheaper or let him pay later. But the druggist said, "No." The husband got desperate and broke into the man's store to steal the drug for his wife. Should the husband have done that? Why? (Kohlberg 1969, 379)

Both Lawrence Kohlberg and Carol Gilligan used this hypothetical situation to elicit individuals' styles and levels of moral reasoning. Gilligan discerned in subjects' responses to this dilemma features of the ethic of care and the ethic of justice that have become the bases of the ideal types of the two ethics.

The first standard distinction drawn between the two moral orientations is their relative abstractness or concreteness. The primary focus of an ethic of justice is a set of abstract principles. In order to act justly in a particular situation we must abstract from the particular features of that situation to see how it comes under a general rule. For instance, we must abstract from individuals' distinguishing features. As Seyla Benhabib puts it, this requires taking the "standpoint of the generalized other," in which we "abstract from the individuality and concrete identity of the other," because "moral dignity is based on what we have in common, not in what differentiates us" (Benhabib 1987, 163–4). In contrast, the ethic of care has as its primary focus the unique and particular features of a situation. For example, rather than abstracting from a person's individuating features, using the ethic of care, we make moral decisions *on the basis of* these features. In Benhabib's language, we take the "standpoint of the concrete other"; "we view every individual as an individual with a concrete history, identity, and affective emotional constitution" (Benhabib 1987, 163–4).

This difference between these approaches can be seen in their responses to the Heinz dilemma. First, however, it is important to note that as it is written the dilemma already abstracts from most of the particular features of its characters, and in this way it is biased toward the ethic of justice. For instance, the dilemma does not reveal anything about the relationship between Heinz and his wife, or about the druggist's motivations in charging Heinz so much for the drug, or about Heinz's wife's wishes. From the justice perspective, it can be argued that these sorts of details are unnecessary: We can tell from the limited information presented that this dilemma represents a conflict between the right to life and the right to property. As one respondent in Gilligan's study put it, the situation can be understood as "a math problem with humans" (Gilligan 1982, 26). Those who approach this dilemma from the justice perspective reach differing conclusions about whether Heinz is justified in stealing the drug, but they are likely to accept the dilemma as presented and to resolve it by fitting the situation under a general rule.

In contrast, those who approach the Heinz dilemma using an ethic of care are generally frustrated by its lack of detail. They are likely to resist the dilemma's attempt to close off all options for getting the drug short of stealing it. Surely, they insist, Heinz could reason with the druggist about the situation. Or he could find a way to borrow more money from friends and family. Or he could hold a bake sale to raise money. Those approaching the dilemma from a care perspective are also likely to worry about whether Heinz will be imprisoned for stealing the drug, thereby abandoning his wife when she needs him most, or whether the drug will really work, or whether Heinz's wife even wants to go on living. From a justice perspective, such questions would reveal an inability to identify the *real* moral issue in the Heinz dilemma but from a care perspective such questions are essential to understanding the situation, and thus to resolving it.

Allied to this abstract/concrete distinction is a distinction between reason and emotion. From the justice perspective, feelings are seen as threatening the universality demanded of moral judgment, and thus we should seek to abstract from our particular feelings and focus on universal principles to be properly moral. As its extreme, in Kant's ethics, an action motivated by feelings, however right it is, has no moral worth. In contrast, from a care perspective, feelings are regarded as morally central. As Emmett Barcalow writes, caring people "rely on their feelings, emotions, natural impulses rather than on rules and principles in deciding what is the right thing to do" (Barcalow 1994, 203). Thus an action motivated by principle, however right it is, has less moral worth than an action arising out of the appropriate feelings of care.

The second standard distinction between the ethic of justice and the ethic of care is based on their different conceptions of the self. The ethic of justice begins with an assumption of human separateness, so that in order to be obligated to others, we must in some sense consent to those obligations.[1] Thus the ethic of justice emphasizes notions of choice and will in understanding our moral obligations. In contrast, the ethic of care begins with an assumption of human connectedness, the result of which is that to a large extent we recognize rather than choose our obligations to others. In other words, the ethic of justice takes freedom as its starting point, while the ethic of care takes obligation as its starting point. This means that the general challenge of the ethic of justice is to show how one's obligations to others arise without violating one's individual autonomy, while the general challenge of the ethic of care is to show how one can achieve individual freedom without violating one's moral obligations to others.

An example might be helpful to show the plausibility of the idea that we have obligations to which we have not consented. Nancy Hirschmann illustrates and defends the view that our obligations are not necessarily grounded in consent by referring to the case of a couple who decide to have child. This voluntary decision would seem to ground the couple's obligations toward the child they create. But suppose the child is born with severe mental or physical disabilities. Assuming that the parents have some obligations toward their disabled child, Hirschmann argues that these obligations should not be understood in terms of consent, as the parents never consented to the situation in which they have found themselves. Rather, the parents *recognize* an obligation that they have not explicitly chosen (Hirschmann 1992, 235).

The different starting points of the two ethics are reflected in two different ways of constructing the problem in the Heinz dilemma. Those using the ethic of justice assume the important question is whether Heinz should steal the drug *as opposed to not stealing it.* Heinz and his wife are, first and foremost, separate individuals, and the question is whether Heinz has this particular obligation to his wife or not. In contrast, those using an ethic of care assume the important question is whether Heinz should steal the drug, *as opposed to getting the drug in some other way.* From this perspective, Heinz and his wife are understood as importantly connected to one another and thus responsible for one another. Thus it is assumed that Heinz has an obligation to help his wife; the question is not *whether* Heinz should help his wife but *how* he should do so. The proposed action of stealing the drug seems irresponsible from the care perspective because it involves severing more connections, when the problem arose in the first place because the druggist severed his connections to the Heinzes by refusing to help them. That is, according to the care perspective, severing connections tends to cause rather than solve moral problems.

This brings me to the third standard distinction between the ethic of care and the ethic of justice, the distinction between their priorities. The ethic of care has two interrelated priorities: maintaining one's relationships and meeting the needs of those to whom one is connected. In contrast, the ethic of justice takes some form of equality as a priority. To be sure, equality is interpreted in different ways in different theories of justice; for example, a libertarian would argue for the equal right to use one's resources as one chooses; a socialist would argue for the equal right to have one's basic needs met; an Aristotelian would argue for returns in proportion to contributions. Libertarians focus on a set of negative rights, socialists on a set of positive rights, and Aristotelians not on rights but duties. Still, all derive these truths from some conception of equality.

These different priorities of care and justice are reflected in different responses to the Heinz dilemma. Those who approach the dilemma using an ethic of justice seek to promote equality as they understand it: some argue that Heinz's actions are wrong because they deprive the druggist of his equal right to use his property as he chooses, while others argue that Heinz's actions are justified because they are necessary to fulfill Heinz's wife's equal right to medical treatment. Conversely, those who interpret the dilemma using the ethic of care hold that Heinz should meet his wife's need for medical treatment but are wary of the solution of stealing the drug because doing so would sever Heinz's relationship to the druggist, and possibly his relationship to his wife as well, if he is caught and imprisoned for his action. Instead, those with a care perspective suggest ways that Heinz might meet his obligation to his wife by drawing upon rather than severing his relationships to others. As the dilemma was constructed, however, Heinz's relations to others would not allow him to provide his wife with the drug she needs, and thus the dilemma rules out the possibility of meeting the priorities of an ethic of care.

So far I have discussed three ways in which the ethic of justice and the ethic of care are usually distinguished. These three distinctions are generally thought to justify two further differences between the ethics that are the source of much of the controversy surrounding the ethics. First, while the ethic of justice is understood to take the concept of autonomy as central, the ethic of care is understood to be opposed to the concept of autonomy on the grounds that it is excessively individualistic. Second, it is typically held that the ethic of justice applies to the public sphere of politics and civil society, while the ethic of care applies to the private sphere of family and friends. I will show how the above three features of the two ethics are thought to result in these characterizations.

First, I will focus on the role of autonomy in the ideal types of care and justice. I will offer an extensive account and defense of an unconventional concept of autonomy in Chapter 2, but here I will refer to a standard notion of autonomy that is typically at issue in the care/justice debate. A general and uncontroversial definition of autonomy is self-determination, or doing what one as an individual has decided to do. Thus an autonomous individual is self-defining, choosing projects and life plans without the interference of outside influences or other people. Autonomous actions are ones that can be said to be truly the agent's own.

Based on their differing assumptions about the role of social relations in constituting an individual's identity, the ethic of justice and the ethic of care reach differing conclusions about autonomy. According to Carol Gilligan, the different images of the self embedded in the two ethics result in different ways of organizing "the basic elements of moral judgment: self, others, and the relationship between them" (Gilligan 1987, 22). Gilligan characterizes these different ways of organizing experience as alternative gestalts, with shifting figures and grounds. From the justice perspective, individual selves are the figures, and moral judgments evaluate the ground—that is, the relationships between individuals—based on the moral ideal of equality. However, from the care perspective, the relationship becomes the figure, while self and other become the ground that is defined by the figure, and moral judgments call for individual response based on the moral ideal of attachment. Whereas the justice perspective takes inequality as its primary cause for moral concern, the care perspective takes detachment as its primary cause for moral concern. From the care perspective, one is able to avoid detachment, or sustain relationships, by recognizing and responding to individuals' needs. In general, then, whereas the justice orientation takes individual identities as fundamental and develops moral injunctions to protect those identities, the care orientation takes relationships as fundamental and develops moral injunctions to protect those relationships.

The ethic of justice's focus on individual identities translates into an emphasis on autonomy. As long as individuals do not interfere with the autonomy of others, they ought to be allowed to define themselves freely. However, the ethic of care's focus on relationships between individuals leads its advocates to be skeptical of the desirability and even the possibility of autonomy. For instance, Gilligan writes that "since the reality of interconnection as experienced by women is given rather than freely contracted, they arrive at an understanding of life that reflects the *limits of autonomy* and control" (Gilligan 1982, 172). She also writes that the ethic of care has "a view of action as responsive and, therefore, as arising in relationship *rather than the view of action as emanating from within the self and, therefore, self-governed*" (Gilligan 1987, 24). That is, since one's identity is to a large degree socially constituted, it would be unrealistic to believe that one could freely define one's own identity.

Although Gilligan believes that the ethic of care does not allow for autonomy, she does not take this to be an indictment of the care orientation; on the contrary, she takes it to be an indictment of the concept of autonomy. For instance, she writes: "Illuminating life as a web rather than a succession of relationships, women portray autonomy rather than attachment as the illusory and dangerous quest" (Gilligan 1982, 48). From a care perspective, autonomy is dangerous because it is maximized through isolation from others, as others represent potential threats to our ability to define ourselves freely. But the more isolated we are, the less we are able to do what the ethic of care values, to create and maintain relationships with particular others. Thus, autonomy is a central value for an ethic of justice while it is generally regarded as illusory or as a negative value by advocates of the ethic of care.

The public/private boundaries of justice and care are more often taken for granted than explicitly defended. But all three standard distinctions between care and justice are understood as implying a division of labor between the two ethics along public/private lines. Those defending the conventional boundaries of justice and care argue that because of the features of the ethic of care, it would be impossible, immoral, or unhelpful to use the ethic in the public sphere.

First, the contextuality of care seems to limit it to situations about which we can know extensive details. We do not know the details of the lives of individuals on the other side of the world, so it would seem impossible for us to care for them. Nel Noddings argues that this is the case. She holds that the contextuality of care means that caring requires real encounters with and responses from individuals. Thus we cannot care for starving children in Africa (if we don't know them), and we cannot care for all humankind. "Caring itself is reduced to mere talk about caring when we attempt to do so" (Noddings 1984, 86). According to Noddings, real caring requires that we not just "care about" but "care for."

> Caring is not simply a matter of feeling favorably disposed toward humankind in general, of being concerned about people with whom we have no concrete connections. There is a fundamental difference between the kind of care a mother has for her child and the kind of 'care' a well-fed American adult has for a starving Somali child s/he has never met. Real care requires actual encounters with specific individuals. (Tong 1993, 110)

According to Noddings, then, the essence of caring—its attention to the uniqueness of the individual cared for—is present only in personal relationships, so "caring" for distant peoples is care in name only.

If, as Noddings argues, we cannot care for people we do not know, it follows that *either* we have no moral obligations toward them *or* our moral obligations toward them are based on something other than care. Critics have argued that Noddings's account of care results in the conclusion that we have *no* obligations to distant peoples. This is because Noddings not only delimits caring to personal relations but defends caring as an alternative to, not merely a complement to justice. As Claudia Card writes, "Resting all of ethics on caring threatens to exclude as ethically insignificant our relationships with most people in the world, because we do not know them and never will" (Card 1990a, 102). Obviously, this is a morally unacceptable conclusion.

In responding to the criticisms of Card and others on this point, Noddings has insisted that she did not mean to suggest that we have no moral obligations to people we do not know. But she has seemed unsure of how to account for these obligations. At times she suggests that her account of caring might be somehow extended to include obligations toward distant people. She offers, for instance, that we might "construct ever-widening circles of care," such that I care for people I meet, who in turn care for people they meet, and so on, until, presumably, everyone is cared for (Noddings 1991, 97). Moreover, recognizing the importance of personal contact in caring, we might press those nearby the distant needy to care for them. In short, at times it looks like Noddings would like her account of caring to be comprehensive but not at the expense of diluting caring so that it does not require personal contact.

At other times, Noddings seems willing to acknowledge that justice is necessary for a comprehensive account of morality. For instance, she writes, "Reducing everything in moral theory to caring is indeed likely to be an error—as are most reductionist attempts—and I did not intend to do this. However, I am not ready to say exactly how justice and care should be combined" (Noddings 1990, 120). Noddings may not be willing to draw the obvious conclusion, but others are: If care is restricted to personal relationships, then all moral obligations beyond personal relations must be based on justice. John Broughton defends Kohlberg against advocates of the ethic of care in writing that justice is "intended as the abstract form that caring takes when respect is maintained and responsibility assumed for people whom one does not know personally and may never come to know" (Broughton 1983, 614).[2] Our moral obligations toward starving children in Africa must be based on abstract principles of justice, according to which, for example, all human beings have a right to have their basic subsistence needs met. The individuating details of these people's lives are both unavailable and irrelevant when we make this judgment: The point is, they are starving and should be fed.

Thus, it has been argued that the first feature of care I have emphasized—its contextuality—requires that care be a personal ethic. Again, this argument holds that because it is impossible to take a contextual perspective in nonpersonal contexts, we must take an abstract perspective. The second feature of care is also thought to rule out the possibility of the ethic of care in non-personal contexts. The ethic of care presupposes the ontological view that the self is socially constituted or defined through its relationships to others. According to this view, *all* individuals, not just those who accept the ethic of care, are socially constituted. Those who accept the ethic of care tend to *experience* themselves as socially constituted and because of this experience, feel an obligation to care for those to whom they feel connected. Yet this experience of social connection is thought to have a limited scope. The recipients of one's care may be one's friends, one's family, or possibly even one's community or nation, but it is hard to imagine that one could experience oneself as connected to all human beings. As Owen Flanagan and Kathryn Jackson argue, citing Hume, it is part of our basic psychological makeup that we have great difficulty widening our "fellow feeling" indefinitely (Flanagan and Jackson 1987, 625). Thus the sense of social connection thought to underlie the ethic of care seems to limit the ethic's scope. According to this argument, since justice does not rely on this social sense,[3] we must turn to rationally grounded theories of justice to ground our moral obligations to those distant and different from us.

Others have allowed that it may be *possible* to use an ethic of care in nonpersonal contexts but have argued that it is nevertheless *unjust* to do so. They have agreed with the above critics that the sense of social connection underlying the ethic of care is limited and have envisioned a public ethic of care based on that sense of social connection. Such an ethic of care would express partiality toward our friends and family members. As Friedman points out, "The infamous 'boss' of Chicago's old-time Democratic machine, Mayor Richard J. Daley, was legendary for his nepotism and political partisanship; he cared extravagantly for his relatives, friends, and political cronies" (Friedman 1987a, 103). Such critics argue that because the ethic of care involves favoritism toward those one is related to, it must be restricted to the sphere of personal relations, where such favoritism is appropriate. To use the Bernard Williams's famous example, a man is allowed (or even required) to save his drowning wife before he saves a drowning stranger (Williams 1981). But, at least in many businesses, it would be morally wrong for that man to *hire* his wife simply because she was his wife. In favoring those close to us, a public ethic of care would be unfair to those outside one's sphere of personal relations.

Others have argued that a political ethic of care would involve partiality toward those we do not know personally, but whom we experience as "like" ourselves in other senses. Joan Tronto writes: "We care more for those who are emotionally, physically, and even culturally closer to us. Thus an ethic of care could become a defense of caring only for one's own family, friends, group, nation. From this perspective, caring could become a justification for any set of conventional relationships" (Tronto 1987, 659). In other words, public versions of the ethic of care, based on a sense of social connection, would seem to endorse clear injustices such as racism or sexism. Therefore we must appeal to the ethic of justice, and its commitment to impartiality, to account for our moral obligations to those we understand as different from us. Rosemarie Tong makes the same point in terms of the abstract/concrete distinction between the two ethics:

> Given the fact that so many social groups knowingly or negligently, willfully or unintentionally, fail to care about those whose sex, race, ethnicity, religion differ from our own, justice must be treasured. Justice often is correctly blind to particulars in order to prevent details of sex, race, and creed from determining whether we care for someone or not. (Tong 1993, 126)

The ethic of care's attention to individual particularities, including the particular relationship between the carer and the person cared for, seem to make it inappropriate as a moral theory for the public sphere. Only an ethic that abstracts from such particularities can avoid unjust favoritism in public decisionmaking.

Finally, some arguments for the restriction of the ethic of care to personal relations focus on the ethic's distinctive priorities: meeting individuals' needs and maintaining one's relationships to others. Critics have argued that such priorities would fail to meet the moral demands of the public sphere, specifically the resolution of conflicting claims, whereas the ethic of justice is specifically designed to address such conflicts. Kohlberg writes that the "ethic of care is, in and of itself, not well-adapted to resolve . . . problems which require principles to resolve conflicting claims among persons, all of whom in some sense should be cared about" (Kohlberg, 1984, 20–21). The ethic of care asks us to meet everyone's needs, but the fact of conflicts over the division of scarce resources, which are the conflicts characteristic of the public sphere, means that not everyone's needs *can* be met. A comprehensive moral theory must offer us fair ways to settle such conflicts, and the ethic of care, with its "warm, mushy and wholly impossible politics of universal love," cannot do so (Ferguson 1984, 172). Broughton also makes this argument: "A principle of help or care does not work in situations where helping one agent harms another. Even in the Heinz dilemma this is a problem; shouldn't Heinz 'care' for the druggist too?" (Broughton 1993, 123). According to Broughton, since it is impossible for Heinz to care for both his wife and the druggist, he must dispense with an ethic of care and make use of an ethic of justice that ranks his wife's right to life against the druggist's right to property.

To summarize, the commonly cited distinguishing features of the ethic of care—its concreteness, its social conception of the self, and its priorities—seem to characterize it as an ethic of personal relations. In some ways, it would be *impossible* to expand the ethic's application beyond personal relations; in other ways it would be *morally wrong* to do so; and in still other ways, it would be *morally unhelpful* to do so.

Although I will not focus on them, corresponding arguments can be made about the role of an ethic of justice in personal or familial contexts. That is, the defining features of the family seem to rule out features of the ethic of justice: the intimacy of family members makes an abstract approach inappropriate; the extent to which our identities are defined by our families makes an individualistic conception of the self inappropriate; and the inherent hierarchy of the family makes the goal of equality inappropriate. The family, it is thought, is beyond justice, and any attempt to reduce the family to justice can only detract from the emotional ties and the common purposes that make the family morally important and unique.[4]

In this chapter I have presented the ideal types of the ethic of care and the ethic of justice. The fact that the two ethics are understood as mutually exclusive of one another has led commentators to focus on particular kinds of questions, such as *which* ethic is better, either in general, or in a particular situation such as the Heinz dilemma. However, as I will argue, it has discouraged commentators from addressing the most important questions surrounding the two ethics, such as how we can distinguish between better and worse versions of each ethic, and how the two ethics are related to one another. In the following chapters, I show some of the limitations and consequences of these ideal types, as well as how we might move beyond them.

Notes

1. Individual theorists who might be understood as defending an ethic of justice would not accept this view. For example, Kant's "will" is not choice, and "consent" is what any rational being *could* will; Kant agrees that we recognize rather than choose our obligations to others. Nevertheless, contractual thinking is an important element in many versions of the ethic of justice, including those of some neo-Kantians such as Rawls. See Held 1987b.

2. I will not examine the claim that this *is* Kohlberg's view but instead the claim that one *could* have such a theory of justice.

3. In Chapter 4, I will argue that it *does*. We apply principles of justice to humans but not usually to non-humans because we experience ourselves as more connected to humans than to nonhumans.

4. See Sandel 1982 for the view that justice is inappropriate in the family.

2

Care and Autonomy

▼

Feminists are divided on the value of an ethic of care. Some view such an ethic not merely as growing out of women's oppression, but also as contributing to the perpetuation of that oppression. Others argue that women's differences from men are potentially sources of strength, and that challenging women's oppression requires valorizing these differences, one of which is the ethic of care. Feminists are also divided on the value of autonomy. Some regard autonomy as an individualistic and masculinist value, one which is both illusory and damaging to women. Others appeal to the notion of autonomy in defending women's right to define themselves according to their own interests and needs.

There are important connections between these two debates. Many feminists who reject the ethic of care do so because they believe it undermines some notion of autonomy. For instance, whereas an autonomous individual defines herself, it is argued that an adherent of the ethic of care allows herself to be defined by others—by those for whom she cares. Similarly, those who criticize the notion of autonomy often do so because they believe it is inconsistent with an ethic of care. For instance, whereas autonomy is thought to be an individualistic notion, the ethic of care is based on the recognition that human beings are socially constituted.

In this chapter, I will show that the view that care and autonomy are mutually exclusive arises from the ideal types of the ethic of care and the ethic of justice, both of which are flawed in important ways. In particular, the usual conception of autonomy is one that arises out of certain individualistic assumptions of the ideal type of the ethic of justice, and these assumptions are incompatible with the ethic of care. However, these individualistic assumptions are not necessary to (or even appropriate for) either the ethic of justice or the concept of autonomy. Thus I will argue that care and autonomy are compatible. This attempt to reconcile care and autonomy is important because, as I shall show, autonomy (properly defined) serves as a criterion for an adequate ethic of care. That is, unless a version of the ethic of care allows for the autonomy of the caregiver and the care recipient, the ethic of care will be deficient on moral and on feminist grounds. Obviously, however, only a nonindividualistic account of autonomy could possibly be compatible with an ethic of care, and I will begin by developing such an account of autonomy.

Before making the argument that, properly understood, care and autonomy are not necessarily mutually exclusive, but can be mutually supportive, I need to acknowledge one limitation of this argument. When I say "properly understood," I mean in part that the care that can be reconciled with autonomy is an ideal version of care. However, there might be important differences between the real care women give and these ideal versions of care which allow for autonomy. If women are not free to choose which of these versions of care they give, it might seem unhelpful to point out that ideally care and autonomy are compatible. In other words, it is quite possible that there is a real tension between autonomy and care that cannot be dissolved simply by proposing a new definition of care. I acknowledge that this is a limitation of this chapter, one that I hope to overcome in the rest of the book, in which I will consider the social changes that must take place if we hope to actualize the ideal version of the ethic of care discussed here. But despite its limitations, I believe this chapter serves an important purpose. Many feminists see a conflict between care and autonomy, and as a result feel obliged to defend care against autonomy or autonomy against care. If it can be shown that there need not be a conflict between care and autonomy, the debate can shift from whether care or autonomy is more important to how we might bring about the social conditions to allow us to overcome their present conflict. I believe that it will be helpful to show that even an ideal version of care is compatible with autonomy.

What Is Autonomy?

Most literally, autonomy means self-determination. An autonomous person is one who is in control of his or her life rather than being controlled by outside forces. As I discussed in Chapter 1, critics of the notion of autonomy have argued that it is impossible to be autonomous based on one of the central insights of the ethic of care, namely that individuals do not create themselves but are, to a large degree at least, socially constituted. In this section, I will define autonomy such that it is not individualistic in a way that conflicts with the social construction of identity. I will show that the fact that we are to a large extent socially constituted does have important implications for our understanding of autonomy. Namely, it reveals that autonomy is not merely an internal, or psychological characteristic, but also an external, or social characteristic. I will argue that when it is understood in this way, it becomes clear that autonomy is not only possible to achieve, but serves as a criterion for an adequate ethic of care.

Most discussions of autonomy regard autonomy as a psychological attribute related to free will, and focus on the impediments to psychological autonomy.

According to standard accounts, there are two general categories of impediments to autonomy, and thus two necessary conditions for achieving autonomy. First, if one is forced to carry out actions which are essentially someone else's actions, one is not autonomous. Thus autonomy requires that one be free of coercion in one's decisionmaking. However, the absence of coercion is not a sufficient condition for autonomy. A choice may be uncoerced yet motivated by ignorance, inner compulsion, or alienation such that the action does not truly represent the agent whose action it is. Thus, in order to ensure that one is self-motivated rather than moved only by social forces, it is necessary that one not only choose for oneself but think reflectively or critically about one's choices. If one has not critically reflected on one's motives, then we cannot be certain that these are one's *own* motives, or, as many philosophers put it, that one's actions have arisen from one's "true" self. Thus a second requirement for autonomy is that one critically reflect on one's choices. Again, as it is usually understood, autonomy has a negative component, that one's choices not be coerced, and a positive component, that one critically evaluate one's choices.[1]

This concept of autonomy is psychological in that it focuses on the sources of the agent's choice which move the agent; that is, on motives, beliefs, values, self-conceptions, and feelings. If the sources of an agent's choice meet the above two conditions, then the agent is thought to be self-determining. However, this conception of autonomy has been challenged on the grounds that meeting these two conditions is still not sufficient to be autonomous. Remember that the primary reason for requiring critical reflection, or higher-order desires, is that our ordinary desires, our first-order desires, are often socially determined. When we reflect on these desires we may realize that they are not really *our* desires. Thus autonomy requires that we take a critical perspective on our socialization. However, perhaps it is not only our first-order desires that are socially constituted, but our higher-order reflections as well; perhaps our critical reflection is itself a social product. If that is the case we seem to lose any right to talk about a "true" self, since a "true" self is generally taken to mean an innate or a self-generated self. If there is no true self, no self which is not determined by its social context, then it would seem to follow that there is no autonomy.

The realization that critical reflection is itself a social product has led philosophers to draw different conclusions. It has led some to search for ways in which the individual can elude his or her socialization and thus be autonomous. These searches generally fail, and thus imply that autonomy is unachievable.[2] However, Diana Meyers suggests that while this debate presents an interesting philosophical puzzle—which is a special case of the free will debate—it is not very helpful in understanding the nature of autonomy.[3] While no one can escape his or her socialization, it is obvious that some people are more autonomous—i.e., in control of their lives—than others. Moreover, without entering into the extensive current debate on autonomy,[4] we can recognize that critical reflection allows people to be more autonomous than they would be otherwise.

Thus there are two approaches that we might take to this question about social constitutiveness and autonomy. On the one hand, we can define autonomy and then consider whether anyone achieves it. On the other hand, we can observe the differences between people we consider autonomous and people we consider nonautonomous, and then make generalizations about what constitutes autonomy. The first approach results in a purer conception of autonomy than the second: The autonomous individual can call everything into question. However, it does so by ruling out the possibility of autonomy; it stalls when it is faced with the fact that we are socially constituted. The second approach results in a more limited, descriptive conception of autonomy, one that accepts the social constitution of the individual. Unlike the first approach, however, this approach is practically helpful in focusing on what allows individuals to control their lives to the extent that they do. For this reason, I will accept the second of these two approaches.

If we are concerned with the conditions that allow individuals to be as in control of their lives as they can be, it becomes obvious that those conditions are not only psychological, but social as well. Therefore, we need to expand upon standard accounts of autonomy. First of all, autonomy cannot be achieved individually. In fact, we *learn* to become autonomous, and we learn this competency not through isolation from others, but through relationships with others. An individual's autonomy is nurtured through the care of others. To understand this it will help to return to the definition of autonomy. Remember that autonomy has not just the negative component of the absence of coercion in one's decisionmaking, but the positive component of critical thinking about one's motives. Isolation may promote the negative component, but it undermines the positive component. For it is the support and guidance of our family, friends and teachers that foster the skills of self-examination allowing us to be autonomous. In other words, relationships with others teach us to be ourselves. As Lorraine Code puts it, "Personal uniqueness, creativity, expressiveness and self-awareness . . . grow out of interdependence, and continually turn back to it for affirmation and continuation" (Code 1987, 361). Of course, some relationships foster these skills better than others and some relationships actually undermine these skills. But relationships, and specifically caring relationships, are a necessary precondition for autonomy.

Other social conditions for autonomy can be understood as expansions of the psychological conditions previously discussed. An individual cannot be said to have control over his or her life without some degree of social power, or ability to carry out his or her decisions. One need not be coerced, in that one is literally forced to carry out someone else's decisions, in order to lack control over one's life. For instance, a battered woman's decision to remain with her batterer may be the best option available to her, but the fact that she makes this decision does not make it an autonomous decision. Or, a nurse may disagree with a physician's decision in a particular case but know from experience that she would risk her liveli-hood if she challenged him, and thus carry out the decision against her wishes. In another sense, one may lack control over one's life to the extent that one is una-ble to take care of oneself, and thus forced to rely on the care of others. Such cases suggest that we need to expand the concept of autonomy to include social conditions that influence the relative capacity of persons to set their own courses, or to do what they decide to do. If we consider only literal coercion as an imped-iment to autonomy, as the psychological account does, then we will overlook a great deal of the factors that influence people's ability to determine their own lives. Thus literal coercion should serve as the limiting case in our understanding of autonomy, and relative power and disempowerment should become the broader issue. Since there are degrees of empowerment, there are also degrees of autonomy.

Critical thinking, the second condition for autonomy, also takes on a broader meaning in light of the social factors that affect our ability to control our own lives. Our culture's influence on our views and perceptions includes, for better or worse, the degree to which we can even imagine being critical of the choices that our culture normally sanctions. For instance, our culture promotes an ideal of femininity that has been defined in terms of self-sacrifice. A young woman in one of Carol Gilligan's studies espouses such an ideal:

> If I could grow up and be like anyone in the world, it would be my mother, because
> I've just never met such a selfless person. She would do anything for anybody, up to
> the point that she has hurt herself a lot because she just gives so much to other peo-
> ple and asks nothing in return. So, ideally, that's what you'd like to be, a person who
> is selfless and giving. (Gilligan 1982, 136)

While this woman seems to be actively thinking about the ideal that she would like to adopt, she is in fact embracing an ideal social role for women without really weighing its possible drawbacks for her mother, for herself, or for women in general. The ability to think about our own decisions critically is largely dependent upon being in a society in which the society's norms which subtly socialize us are critically analyzed and discussed. This means that voices that challenge the status quo must be allowed or even encouraged to exist and to be heard in a social discourse on important social values. This discourse must be available to the average person, and society must be set up in a way that citizens are able to effect political change based on this discourse. There are degrees of critical capacity, and thus degrees of autonomy, but it is clear that our critical capacities are maximized in social conditions that permit and encourage us to critically assess and influence the social ideals that in turn shape our lives. For instance, the extent to which young women today are critical of the ideal of fem-ininity as self-sacrificing is largely the result of their exposure to and participation in recent cultural and political discourse on issues affecting women.

Thus, while certain psychological conditions are certainly necessary for autonomy, we cannot understand autonomy by focusing on psychological factors alone. In some ways psychological autonomy depends on social conditions that are usually unacknowledged. As I have discussed, certain social conditions make it possible for us to develop the capacity to control our lives to the extent that we can. Moreover, psychological conditions are not sufficient to account for autonomy, for one may be psychologically autonomous yet socially disempowered to an extent that one cannot be said to have control over one's life. Thus, each of the two standard conditions for autonomy—the absence of coercion and the skill of critical thinking—need to be expanded to incorporate social factors. In the first instance, literal cases of coercion are not the only impediments to autonomy; in addition, different forms of disempowerment impede autonomy to varying degrees. In the second case, an individual's critical thinking capacity cannot be understood simply as an individual trait; social conditions serve to impede or to nurture this trait, and thus they must be included in a complete account of autonomy.

Again, advocates and critics of the ethic of care often focus their disagreement on the concept of autonomy. While its advocates claim that the ethic of care is superior to the ethic of justice because it does away with the concept of autonomy, its critics claim that the ethic of care is deficient because it compromises women's autonomy. But broadening our account of autonomy to include social factors eliminates the excessive individualism that conflicts with the ethic of care. It also allows us to focus on the core of the feminist criticism of the ethic of care, namely that it serves to disempower women. I think it is self-evident that if the ethic of care *does* undermine its adherents' autonomy, or their relative capacity to make and carry out their own decisions, then the ethic of care is self-destructive for women and should be criticized on feminist grounds. This will serve as one of two general criteria I will use in critically examining the ethic of care in this work.

It might be objected that because of its other-orientation, caring necessarily (and rightfully) rules out *self*-determination. But the notion of autonomy I defend would certainly not conflict with being a caregiver; instead, it would seek to empower caregivers by demanding that they have the power to carry out their responsibilities adequately, as they often do not. The ethic of care *would* inevitably threaten autonomy if autonomy required that one be able to consent to one's own obligations, but most versions of the ethic of justice would likewise threaten such an account of autonomy.[5] Similarly, if autonomy means that one is able do what one *wants* to do, the ethic of care will threaten autonomy, as caring requires making sacrifices for the other. But such a concept of autonomy will be threatened by nearly any moral theory, and certainly by any adequate moral theory. The question I will address is whether adherents of the ethic of care, who are typically women, are systematically disempowered, *relative to adherents of the ethic of justice*, who are typically men.

In the next two sections, I will examine two attempts to reconcile autonomy and care, one from the individualistic perspective associated with the ethic of justice, and the other from the social perspective associated with the ethic of care. I will show that these accounts reveal some important features of the relationship between care and autonomy but that they also reveal some of the dangers of the ideal types of the two ethics.

An Individualistic Approach to Care and Autonomy

In this section I will consider one attempt to show the importance of autonomy to an adequate ethic of care. This view arises out of the recognition that caring relationships are often damaging to either the caregiver or to the recipient of care, and that threats to autonomy are a central form of this damage. According to this account, *genuine* care requires the autonomy of both the caregiver and the recipient. Caregivers must be *self-asserting* rather than *self-effacing*. Care is *distorted* whenever it compromises the autonomy of the recipient or the caregiver. In this section, I will also show how this account makes these connections between autonomy and care. On a general level, this account reconciles autonomy and care by arguing that autonomy must underlie care: genuine caring relationships take place between autonomous individuals and serve to promote their autonomy.

While this account shows the ways in which care is diminished when it is not grounded in autonomy, I will show that it is limited by the individualistic assumptions that tend to accompany the ethic of justice. In particular, these assumptions contradict the nature of caregiving by understanding the paradigmatic caring relationship as one between autonomous parties and by characterizing interests as individualistic.

Care that threatens its recipient's autonomy is distorted almost by definition, since the purpose of care is to help its recipient, and since autonomy is a good thing. The connection between the autonomy of the caregiver and the quality of care requires more argument. In one of the best defenses of this approach, Lawrence Blum, Marcia Homiak, Judy Housman and Naomi Scheman write: "Concern, care, and support may be defective unless they are founded on a strong sense of autonomy or independence and a healthy concern for oneself, so that in some sense a genuine and non-defective care actually requires autonomy" (Blum et al. 1975, 224). According to this account, two components of care are compromised by the absence of autonomy on the part of the carer. First, and most simply, care requires a commitment to helping or nurturing the recipient of care the best one can. This helping in turn requires a second component of care, namely that the carer is able to understand the recipient of care in his or her own terms.[6] As Nel Noddings defines it, caring involves "apprehending the reality of the other," the "engrossment in another, a putting aside of self and entering as far as possible into the experience of another" (Grimshaw 1986, 216). Similarly, Sheila Mullett defines care as the cultivated "ability to apprehend the world through the eyes of another" (Mullett 1988, 122). Here the claim is that an autonomous individual is best able to apprehend the reality of the other and thus to help the other. I note that there might seem to be a tension between these two components of care. As I will show, helping another the best we can sometimes involves challenging his own terms, rather than accepting him on his terms. Thus it is important to distinguish between *apprehending* the reality of the other and *accepting* the reality of the other. In order to help the other the best we can, we must apprehend, but not necessarily accept the other's reality.[7] I will focus on these two components of care separately, showing how each requires autonomy.

First, according to this account, if a carer lacks autonomy, her care will be less helpful than it would be otherwise. Blum et al. (1975) make this point when they explore the dynamics of a traditional marriage and show that this relationship distorts care, despite the fact that it provides our paradigm case of care. It does so because it denies the wife autonomy. The authors state that two features of such a marriage disempower the woman. First, she is economically dependent on her husband, and second, it is seen as her role "to provide emotional support nonreciprocally for her husband" (Blum et al. 1975, 230). In this relationship it is understood that the husband's role is to provide economic security, while the wife's role is to provide emotional support by meeting her husband's emotional needs which are frustrated at work. As the authors note, this understanding tends to be maintained even when both spouses work outside the home. Although Blum et al. focus on economic dependence, similar claims could be made about emotional dependence, and I will interpret the following arguments as applying to dependence generally.

Blum et al. explain that these features of marriage compromise a wife's autonomy in that they ensure that her care for her husband generally cannot take forms which are threatening to his views or self-concept; offering care of this sort would threaten her own well-being. On the surface, however, this restriction would not seem to compromise care, for care is intended to support rather than to threaten the recipient of care. But the authors hold that supporting someone sometimes requires threatening his views or self-concept. They illustrate with the case of a scientist who cannot get along with his coworkers because of his need to dominate them, and whose supportive wife accepts his rationalization that his coworkers are incompetent. Genuine or self-asserting care would require a challenge to his destructive sense of self-importance (Blum et al. 1975, 231). But the wife's limited and dependent role in the marriage makes such a challenge difficult; thus it causes her to offer a distorted form of care.

The authors allow that the forms of care permitted within this relationship are often helpful to the husband. For instance, because of his wife's support and encouragement, a man may overcome his insecurities and succeed in difficult and competitive work. Also, a wife may be able to manipulate her husband's behavior without expressing criticism of him—for instance, by advising him to adapt to his coworkers' inadequacies. This manipulation, however, will help her husband only in a superficial sense, and will hurt him by giving him a distorted view of himself. So although this wife's self-effacing care can be somewhat helpful to her husband, it is not as helpful as the care that could be given by a wife who was not coerced into refraining from expressing her criticisms.

So far I have focused on the ways in which traditional marriage undermines a woman's autonomy by constraining her choices. But Blum et al. also hold that such a marriage goes further by undermining a wife's autonomy in a second sense, by undermining her capacity for critical thought. "As she becomes accustomed to being dependent on her husband her sense that she is even capable of independence may well begin to disappear" (Blum et al. 1975, 231). This further erosion of her autonomy will distort her care even more.

This brings us to the second component of care. Care not only requires a commitment to helping the other, but in order to achieve this end it typically requires a capacity to "apprehend the reality of the other." That is, I can best help you if I understand you in your own terms. The empathy that it requires to understand another person in his or her own terms is often associated with the feminine experience of feeling connected to others. Nancy Chodorow describes this experience and contrasts it with the masculine experience of feeling separate from others:

> Girls come to experience themselves as continuous with others; their experience of self contains more flexible or permeable ego boundaries. Boys come to define themselves as more separate and distinct, with a greater sense of rigid ego-boundaries and differentiation. The basic feminine sense of self is connected with the world; the basic masculine sense of self is separate. (Chodorow 1978, 169)

It is usually thought that this feeling of connectedness allows women to be especially good at empathizing with others, at apprehending their realities. But according to this account, there is an important sense in which women's experience of connectedness works *against* this end. It does so insofar as it prevents an individual from distinguishing between her own identity and the identity of others. In order to understand you in your own terms, I must understand who you are, *as opposed to who I am*. Jean Grimshaw explains:

> If I see myself as "indistinct" from you, or you as not having your own being that is not merged with mine, then I cannot preserve a real sense of your well-being as opposed to mine. Care and understanding require the sort of distance that is needed in order not to see the other as a projection of the self, or self as a continuation of the other. (Grimshaw 1986, 183)

Here Grimshaw suggests two explanations for why I may not be able to distinguish between my own identity and the identity of others. On the one hand, I may define myself in terms of the other, by, for instance, taking on my husband's interests as my own. As I have discussed, this identification with another person's interests is morally problematic if it is done completely and thus uncritically. Genuine care for another person requires that one retain one's own individual identity.

On the other hand, I may not be able to distinguish between my own identity and that of others because I have defined others in my own terms. Marilyn Frye (1983) explores this phenomenon by drawing a distinction between the "arrogant eye" and the "loving eye." The arrogant eye sees everything with reference to its own interests. It cannot conceive of the separateness of other people, of the fact that others have their own purposes which do not concern it. The other cannot be independent; its purpose is, or must be made to be, to serve the arrogant perceiver. According to Frye, men have had the institutional power to impose this vision on others, limiting women's options so that accepting the arrogant perceiver's view that their purpose is to serve men is the most desirable option. (Frye 1983, 67) Thus the arrogant eye operates through denying the independence of the other, which obviously precludes caring for the other in his or her own terms.

Although Frye describes the arrogant eye as a masculine approach, we can see a feminine version of it as well in the substitute success syndrome. As Blum et al. show, because of their own frustrated ambitions, some wives have not only supported their husband's careers, but have transferred their own ambitions to their husbands and their careers, substituting their husbands' success for their own. This distorted care can be harmful to the husband by pushing him in directions that are in line with his wife's frustrated ambitions but are inappropriate for him. We also see the substitute success syndrome in relationships between some mothers and children:

> [When a mother] does not have a strong sense of self, she will be unable to separate her needs from [her children's] needs and they too may fail to recognize that they are striving toward goals which reflect her values and choices rather than their own. (Blum et al. 1975, 238)

Like the arrogant perceiver, the restricted wife does not understand her husband and children in their own terms, but in terms of her interests. Of course, her relative powerlessness results in an important difference between her and the arrogant perceiver as well: She does not define her husband and children in terms of service to her. Instead she asks them to lead the life she wishes she could lead. Because she does not acknowledge their independence, her care for them is distorted. Analogously, charity has sometimes been criticized as a distorted form of care. For instance: "Though charity might be motivated by a genuine concern for the other, this concern takes a distorted form in that charity reinforces and expresses a sense of inferiority and lack of autonomy in the recipient" (Blum et al. 1975, 246).

In all of these cases we see that care for the other, in the sense of apprehending their reality, is possible only when the carer and the recipient of care are recognized

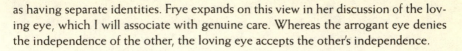

as having separate identities. Frye expands on this view in her discussion of the loving eye, which I will associate with genuine care. Whereas the arrogant eye denies the independence of the other, the loving eye accepts the other's independence.

> One who sees with a loving eye is separate from the other whom one sees. There are boundaries between them; she and the other are two; their interests are not identical; they are not blended in vital parasitic or symbiotic relations, nor does she believe they are or try to pretend they are. (Frye 1983, 75)

Thus the loving eye requires "being able to tell one's own interests from those of others and . . . knowing where one's self leaves off and another begins" (Frye 1983, 75). In a genuinely caring relationship, one cannot define the other in terms of oneself, nor can one define oneself in terms of the other: Genuine care can only take place between autonomous beings who are recognized as such.

This brings me to my criticism of the view that care requires autonomy, namely that it rests on an unrealistic model of care. Specifically, it is unrealistic to expect that all parties in a caring relationship be autonomous. First, it might be argued that it is unrealistic to require autonomy of the carer, but as I argued earlier, even if this is the case, this requirement is not necessarily problematic. It is an ideal that we have not yet achieved. However, I want to argue that the requirement that the recipient of care should be autonomous is unrealistic in a different way. In many cases the recipient of care is not and cannot be autonomous. For instance, this model cannot easily accommodate care for children; it only appears to do so by somehow "promoting" the nonautonomous recipient of care so that he or she appears autonomous. As Annette Baier writes, "Children are treated as adults-to-be, the ill and dying are treated as continuers of their earlier more potent selves" (Baier 1987a, 33). In other words, on this model the "normal" person is autonomous. There is something so normal about autonomy that even individuals who are not autonomous are treated as in some sense autonomous.

This model of caring relationships as based on the autonomy of both parties is actually part of a more general model of moral relationships taking place between equals who freely choose to participate in these relationships. On this model, dependence of any kind is a negative. For instance, Simone de Beauvoir writes that "the ideal . . . would be for entirely self-sufficient human beings to form unions with one another only in accordance with the untrammeled dictates of their mutual love" (de Beauvoir 1952, 490). Ultimately then, according to this view, only autonomous, equal individuals who freely choose to enter into a relationship with each other can genuinely care for one another.

In fact, however, one of the main reasons we need to care for others is because they are *not* autonomous, and a great many of our caring relationships are with individuals who are not autonomous. Child care is one of the central caring relationships in most people's lives. Moreover, in most of our relationships, both parties are not equally powerful, and many of our caring relationships are not freely entered into. For instance, though we may choose to have children, we do not choose to have parents. Why then should we take autonomous individuals as the paradigmatic recipients of care? We should do so, according to this account, in order to rule out distorted versions of care which undermine the autonomy of its recipients. However, this model is only helpful when the recipient of care is at least potentially autonomous. But in many cases autonomy cannot function as an ideal. For instance, even though child care should promote children's eventual autonomy, it doesn't make much sense to say that *ideally* children would be adults. In other cases, such as caring for individuals who are severely mentally retarded, it makes even less sense; often the recipients of care are and will remain unavoidably nonautonomous.

This model is unrealistic about the recipients of care because it begins with certain problematic assumptions about the nature of individual identity. It assumes, for instance, that individuals are "naturally" autonomous unless they are interfered with by others. Presumably children naturally *become* autonomous unless they are interfered with by others. For instance, Shulamith Firestone writes that "the best way to raise a child is to lay off" (Grimshaw 1986, 142). As Lorraine Code puts it, this account assumes "that human beings grow naturally to autonomous self-sufficiency, only then—perhaps cautiously, incidentally, or as an afterthought—to engage in close relationships" (Code 1987, 363). As I discussed in the previous section, however, autonomy is a competency that is nurtured through relationships with others.

We can illustrate this point by returning to the marriage described earlier. In such a marriage, a wife's autonomy is undermined by the fact that her husband doesn't reciprocate her care. Caring is her job, not his, so she does not feel justified in asking him to support her as she supports him. In contrast, a husband's autonomy is supported by his wife's caregiving. The myth of such a marriage is that the wife is dependent, while the husband is independent. Of course both husband and wife are dependent on one another, but, as Catherine Keller puts it, "the task of one is to assert its apparent independence, the task of the other is to support that appearance" (Keller 1986, 8). That is, he is dependent upon her care for his sense of independence. And if Blum et al. are correct that her care is possible only if she is autonomous, then her care is in the end dependent on the care given her by others. Thus the assumption that individual autonomy can be assumed as a starting point must be rejected. Only as a result of the care of others can an individual become autonomous.

Some commentators have interpreted this account's emphasis on individual autonomy as an endorsement of selfishness. For instance, Bernice Fisher and Joan Tronto interpret Blum et al. as addressing themselves to the problem that caring is a burden for women, and as proposing as a solution to that problem that women put their own needs first (Fisher and Tronto 1990, 35). But if everyone put his or her needs and interests first, this would seem to rule out the possibility of an ethic of care. In the following passage, Naomi Scheman argues that such egoism would lead to a breakdown of caretaking and long-term relationships.

> There is every reason to react with alarm to the prospect of a world filled with self-actualizing persons pulling their own strings, capable of guiltlessly saying "no" to anyone about anything, and freely choosing when to begin and end all their relationships. It is hard to see how, in such a world, children could be raised, the sick or disturbed could be cared for, or people could know each other through their lives and grow old together. (Scheman 1983, 240)

In other words, an ethic of care often requires that we subordinate our own individualistically defined interests to those of others. By recommending selfishness, these writers argue, Blum et al. undermine the possibility of developing an ethic of care.

I want to defend this account against the criticism that it undermines care by recommending selfishness. Although Blum et al. do recommend "a healthy concern for oneself," they do so as a precondition for the possibility of caring for others, and they convincingly show that care suffers when the carer does not retain a certain degree of self-interest. Insofar as self-interest is recommended, it is recommended not for its own sake, but for the sake of care, so this self-interest cannot be called selfish. Therefore, if their arguments succeed in showing that autonomy is a precondition for care, they cannot be interpreted as recommending selfishness.

Conversely, there is another sense in which "putting your own interests first" is incompatible with an ethic of care. This is the case if "your own interests" are taken to be sharply distinct from "the interests of others," or in other words, if one maintains what Grimshaw calls an individualism of interests (Grimshaw 1986, 141). Frye in particular lends herself to such an interpretation by writing that "though anyone might wish, for any of many reasons, to contribute to another's pursuit of his or her interests, the health and integrity of an organism is a matter of its being organized largely toward its own interests and welfare" (Frye 1983, 69–70). In this passage, Frye allows that one may choose to help another person, but not because the other's interests are in some sense one's own interests. One's own interests are not defined in terms of the interests of others. Each individual's interests remain distinct from those of others. Such an individualism threatens an ethic of care because care requires more than helping the other when it serves one's own purposes to do so. It requires a greater sense of connection between the self and other, or the sense that the well-beings of the self and other are linked, so that, as Joy Kroeger-Mappes puts it, "acting in the interest of others is also to act in the interest of oneself" (Kroeger-Mappes 1991a, 12). This means that no sharp distinction can be drawn between the interests of the self and the interests of the other. One's own interests include the interests of those one cares for, although, as I argued earlier, the two identities remain distinct. The version of care that Frye allows for does not include this sense of connection.

It might be thought that I have misinterpreted this emphasis on separateness, that in fact Frye's view does allow for carers' interests to include the interests of others. It does not allow for carers' interests to be *identical* to the interests of others: If a carer does not retain an individual identity, her care will be distorted. Thus the claim is only that our interests are not identical, not that there is no overlap between our interests. But I don't think that Frye's position can avoid an individualism of interests this easily. In the following passage, she explicitly defends an individualism of interests. "Cooperation is essential, of course, but it will not do that I arrange everything so that you get enough exercise: for me to be healthy, I must get enough exercise. My being adequately exercised is logically independent of your being so" (Frye 1983, 70). Of course, Frye is right about the logical independence of each individual's physical health, but she is wrong to use physical health as a model for interests in general. Most interests are not logically independent in this sense. For instance, the mental health of an individual is not logically independent of the mental health of those he or she is related to. Thus a carer's interest in mental health cannot be sharply distinguished from the interest in mental health of those he cares for.

Perhaps Frye has taken her argument to an unnecessary extreme; fundamentally, this view requires only that a carer retain a sense of self distinct from the recipients of her care. The view need not be committed to the individualism of interests, only to the nonidentity of interests. I think this is right, but I also think that there is a reason Frye takes the view too far, and that is that she makes certain unstated assumptions.

Specifically, she makes the liberal assumption that human beings are first and foremost individuals, and only secondarily social beings. The true self is an inner core that is distinct from the social self (Grimshaw 1986, 142). This means that if our interests include the interests of others, it is because we choose to enter into relationships with them. But in fact we are related to others whether we like it or not. We are defined by our relationships to others; we are socially constituted. Being socially constituted means more than being a social being, or having relationships with others. I have claimed that it is only through the care of others that individuals learn to be autonomous. But being socially constituted means more than being socialized. The social dimension is fundamental to an individual's autonomy not just developmentally, but logically. As Jennifer Nedelsky puts it, "the content of one's law is comprehensible only with reference to shared norms, values, and concepts" (Nedelsky 1989, 11). More generally, there is no such thing as a separate individual. We can only make sense of our own experiences through concepts which themselves make sense only in a social framework.

In sum, this account is valuable in several ways. It shows that care need not be abandoned as a mere symptom of women's oppression. It also reminds us that care which undermines the autonomy of its recipient is distorted. However, this approach makes assumptions about individual identity that are not only false but which deny the role of care in our lives. For example, this approach assumes that individuals are naturally autonomous, when in fact individuals become autonomous as a result of the care others give them. This approach also tends to presuppose an individualism of interests, which conflicts with the ethic of care's insight that our interests are interdependent and, more generally, that we are socially constituted.

A Social Approach to Care and Autonomy

In the last section we found that the individualistic assumptions that tend to accompany the ethic of justice rule out certain important features of the ethic of care. Lorraine Code writes:

> It makes a difference whether one moves from autonomy to community, or in the opposite direction .... Theorists who take communality and interdependence as their starting point seem better able to accommodate the requirements of autonomy than theorists who take autonomous existence as the "original position" are able to accommodate the requirements of community. (Code 1987, 360)

In this section, I will follow Code's advice and try a new starting point. In the accounts that I considered in the previous section, care was defined as having two components: apprehending the reality of the other, and helping the other the best one can. But the care I will consider in this section will be an ethic of care based on a relational ontology. As we will see, this relational ontology is connected to a priority of sustaining one's relationships with others. I will consider an attempt to reconcile autonomy and care by showing that in its most developed form, the ethic of care yields its own version of autonomy. This attempt depends on yet another component of care that is found at the highest level of the ethic of care, namely including oneself as an object of care. I will examine the success of this attempt to reconcile autonomy and care by focusing on situations in which sustaining a relationship is detrimental to oneself.

I will show that the relational ontology of the ethic of care is interpreted in ways that have both positive and negative results for the caregiver's autonomy. On the one hand, recognizing the extent to which our interests are interdependent with those we care for allows us to find ways to meet the needs of self *and* other, rather than one at the other's expense. On the other hand, the ethic of care's relational ontology has been interpreted as implying an overriding moral obligation to maintain one's relationships to others, which undermines the carer's autonomy. I will argue that the ethic of care can allow for autonomy if it instead prioritizes maintaining (and creating) *healthy* relationships with others.

As I have discussed, advocates of the ethic of care tend to define autonomy as individualistic and locate it in the justice perspective. However, there are a number of indications that Carol Gilligan believes that the care perspective provides its own version of autonomy arising out of its social conception of the self. At least once she makes this explicit, writing that from the care perspective, "the concept of autonomy is changed," and adding that "the seeming paradox 'taking charge of yourself by looking at others around you' conveys the relational dimension of the self-initiated action" (Gilligan 1986b, 241). To see how the ethic of care might offer its own conception of autonomy, we need to look at the stages of this ethic in more detail.

Gilligan divides the ethic of care into three increasingly adequate stages. At the first stage of the ethic of care, one cares strictly for oneself in order to ensure one's own survival (Gilligan 1986a , 318). For instance, at this stage a teenage girl who finds herself pregnant and alone resorts to abortion as an act of self-protection. The transition to the second stage of the ethic of care takes place when one begins to recognize a connection between self and others, and as a result comes to regard the earlier focus on one's own needs as selfish. At the second stage, one shifts one's focus from oneself to others, adopting a feminine conception of goodness as self-sacrifice. Here one seeks to avoid hurting those to whom one is related by deferring to their wishes. It is important to recognize that the woman at the second stage of care, like the woman at the first stage, does not take responsibility for her actions in a morally significant way. She is not autonomous. Even if she is not coerced in her choices, she does not bring a critical perspective to her decisions. Her motives are simply given to her by her social situation; she does not choose them.

However, with the transition from the second to the third stage, the adherent of the ethic of care begins to take responsibility for her choices. This transition takes place when one realizes that denying one's own needs is in fact a violation of the responsibility to care:

> When the conventions of feminine goodness legitimize only others as the recipients of moral care, the logical inequality between self and other and the psychological violence that it engenders create the disequilibrium that initiates the second transition. (Gilligan 1986a, 318)

At the third stage, then, the self is for the first time considered of equal worth to the other. This allows one to conceive of responsibility in a new way, recognizing that it is not selfish but responsible to attend to one's own needs, and that selflessness is actually irresponsible. It is irresponsible, first of all, because it hurts oneself as an individual. It may also contribute to the breakdown of one's relationships with others, insofar as sustaining connections requires acting responsively toward both others and self. As Gilligan writes, "the exclusion of self, like the exclusion of others, renders relationships lifeless by dissolving the fabric of connection. With this dissolution, attachment becomes impossible" (Gilligan 1986b, 251). Thus recognizing an equality between self and other allows one to overcome earlier tensions between selfishness and responsibility. Care requires that one attend to the needs of both self and other, not one to the exclusion of the other. In attending to one's own needs, one is honest to oneself and thus able to take responsibility for one's decisions.

In taking responsibility for one's decisions, one is autonomous. Gilligan supports this interpretation when she writes of the third level of care:

> Now the conventions which in the past had guided her moral judgment become subject to a new criticism, as she questions not only the justification for hurting others in the name of morality but also the "rightness" of hurting herself. However, to sustain such criticism in the face of conventions that equate goodness with self-sacrifice, the woman must verify her capacity for independent judgment and the legitimacy of her own point of view. (Gilligan 1986b, 327)

Gilligan does not use the word "autonomy" here, but she is clearly describing the concept of autonomy. At the third level of the ethic of care, one must have a well-developed critical capacity, one which calls into question social conventions according to which a "good" woman sacrifices her own interests for those of others. Diana Meyers picks up on this suggestion in Gilligan's work, and formulates the test for this version of autonomy as "determining whether or not one could avow responsibility for an act while retaining one's self-respect" (Meyers 1987b, 150). One retains one's self-respect by recognizing the legitimacy of one's own point of view, but also by ensuring the legitimacy of one's own point of view by critically examining it. Thus one brings one's critical perspective not only to social conventions but to one's own point of view. If this is a valid interpretation of Gilligan, then she too implicitly defends a version of autonomy that arises out of the universalization of the injunction to care. On this view, autonomy is not in conflict with the ethic of care, but is actually the fulfillment of it.

However, it is not obvious that the independent judgment Gilligan requires at the highest level of the ethic of care is an adequate conception of autonomy. This is because of one of the general features of the ethic of care, at least in its ideal type. Remember that for the care orientation sustaining one's relationships is a fundamental priority. Detachment is the primary cause for moral concern. In fact, one can understand the responsibility to recognize and respond to individuals' needs as derived from the fundamental responsibility to sustain one's relationships. For instance, Nel Noddings argues that it can never be caring to end a relationship. She says that it may be necessary to one's physical or psychological well-being to do so but that it can never be caring, which for her means that it can never be moral (Noddings 1990b, 124–125).

However, this focus on sustaining one's relationships poses an obvious impediment to autonomy. Autonomy requires that one critically examine one's choices; thus an ethic which requires that one refrain from critically examining one of one's choices—namely, the choice to remain in a particular relationship—cannot allow for autonomy. An autonomous individual must be able to critically examine her involvement in a relationship and choose to withdraw from it or diminish her commitment to it. As Joan Tronto writes, "If the preservation of a web of relationships is the starting premise of an ethic of care, then there is little basis for critical reflection on whether those relationships are good, healthy, or worthy of preservation" (Tronto 1987, 660). It is especially important for a feminist ethics to recognize this because women are often involved in physically or psychologically abusive relationships, and they often feel more commitment to the relationship than to their own well-being. As Blum et al. describe, women's concern for relationships is often "deflected from the content of the relationship to the bare preservation of its form. 'For the sake of her marriage' she overlooks problems, excuses faults, suppresses anger, feigns sexual pleasure, and ignores or lies about any beginnings of dissatisfaction" (Blum et al. 1975, 241). A feminist ethic of care must allow its adherents to take a critical perspective on their relationships, but the care orientation seems to rule this out. Thus the care orientation seems to rule out autonomy.

Gilligan responds to this criticism in two different ways. First, she argues that given certain features of the third level of the ethic of care, the focus on sustaining one's relationships does not undermine autonomy. Second, she argues that at the third level of the ethic of care, sustaining one's relationships is de-emphasized. I will argue that the first response is helpful in some ways but fails to solve the problem, while the second response solves the problem by moving away from the ideal type of the ethic of care.

Gilligan's first response, then, is to point to an important feature of the third stage of the ethic of care. At the second stage, an individual recognizes her connection to others, specifically by recognizing her responsibilities to others. But here she still sees an irreducible tension between her own interests and those of others: She can either satisfy her own needs and be selfish, or satisfy others' needs and be responsible, but not both. However, the transition from the second to the third stage is based on an increased understanding of the interconnection between self and others that allows one to dissipate the tension between caring for oneself and caring for others (Gilligan 1982, 74). This understanding of one's interconnection to others allows one to see conflicts between self and other "as arising from a faulty construction of reality" (Gilligan 1986a, 329). According to Gilligan, then, a true understanding of one's connection to others allows one to reconstruct reality in such a way that caring for self and caring for others is connected rather than opposed.

Specifically, conflicts between self and other can be overcome if one recognizes the depth of one's interdependence to others. Although from the justice perspective, organized by the dimensions of equality and inequality, dependence means powerlessness, from the care perspective, organized by the dimensions of attachment and detachment, dependence

> no longer means being helpless, powerless and without control; rather it signifies a conviction that one is able to have an effect on others, as well as the recognition that *the interdependence of attachment empowers both the self and the other, not one at the other's expense.* (Gilligan 1986b, 249)

Gilligan's claim is that the care orientation's understanding of interdependence allows us to find moral solutions that would be unavailable otherwise. She illustrates by distinguishing between the fair solutions of the justice perspective and the inclusive solutions of the care perspective. "Whereas the fair solution protects identity and ensures equality within the context of a relationship, the inclusive solution transforms identity through the experience of a relationship" (Gilligan 1986b, 243). Thus while the mere existence of a moral problem rules out an inclusive solution if individual identities are taken as givens, an inclusive solution may be possible if individual identities are recognized as socially constituted.

Gilligan illustrates with a story of two four-year-old children playing together:

> In this particular version of a common dilemma, the girl said, "Let's play next-door neighbors." "I want to play pirates," the boy replied. "Okay," said the girl, "then you can be the pirate that lives next door." (Gilligan 1986b, 242)

The girl offers an inclusive solution, one that recognizes the way in which individual interests are created, or at least transformed by social relationship.[8] "The relationship between the children gives rise to a game that neither had separately imagined" (Gilligan 1986b, 243). In contrast, the solution that the justice perspective would offer the children—of taking turns playing each game—leaves individual interests intact. As a result it is not an inclusive solution, but a compromise. Again, inclusive solutions, or solutions that find a way to integrate the needs of self and other, are made possible by a new understanding of the interconnection between self and other.

I have argued that the independent judgment required by the third stage of care can qualify as autonomy only if it allows one to call into question relationships which conflict with one's individual needs. But in her reinterpretation of dependence, Gilligan suggests that there is no need to call our relationships into question. This is because the reconstruction of reality entailed by the third stage instead calls such *conflicts* into question by emphasizing the extent to which we are constituted by our relationships—that is, the extent to which we do not have separable individual needs.

Nel Noddings takes up this line of argument even more explicitly. Those who worry that the ethic of care might work against women's interests are, according to Noddings, presupposing a mistaken individualistic conception of self. She writes:

> I do not give and receive in kind as a totally separate individual. Rather my individuality—my social self—is defined in relation. . . . Therefore, when I do something for someone else, I enhance myself through the relation that defines me as well as the other. (cited in Houston 1990, 117)

Here Noddings takes the view that because one is defined by one's relationships, caring *cannot* be self-sacrificing. Giving to one's relationships can only benefit oneself. More generally, this line of thinking suggests that if individuals are constituted by their relationships to one another, their well-beings cannot be at odds.

I grant that recognizing one's interdependence allows one to find solutions to moral problems which integrate the needs of self and other, solutions that would not be available otherwise. But not all needs can be integrated. In many cases, the needs of one member of a relationship directly conflict with those of another member. For instance, as some women interpret the Heinz dilemma, Heinz must choose between allowing his wife to die or going to jail himself as a result of stealing the drug for her. Or, to take a more realistic example, many women's needs to work outside the home conflict with the needs among other members of the family—for a stay-at-home wife and mother or a homemaker. In fact, Gilligan says that one of the conflicts that women at the third stage seek to resolve is that between femininity and adulthood, which is expressed as the conflict between commitments to family and to work (Gilligan 1986a, 333). Her implication is that there is some way of reconstructing reality, or something one can know, which will resolve this conflict. But this conflict is not the result of a misunderstanding; family and work do make conflicting demands on women (Auerbach et al. 1981).

Not only is the suggestion that inclusive solutions can be found for all conflicts wrong but it is also damaging to women. As Gilligan acknowledges, women often find it difficult to take moral stands, and this is not only because they resist the typical presentation of moral dilemmas abstracted from context. It is also because they experience themselves as powerless: "These women's reluctance to judge stems from their uncertainty about their right to make moral statements, or perhaps from the price for them that such judgment seems to entail" (Gilligan 1982, 66). Self-assertion may cost them the relationship, on which they are dependent in more than one way: "Her very real dependence on his continuing economic and social support may well make her more reluctant to bring up with him, or even, often, to confront in herself, problems and dissatisfaction" (Blum et al. 1975, 241).

If women are already reluctant to assert themselves, and they believe that they *should* be able to integrate everyone's interests, it seems unlikely that they will assert their own interests against those of others. Instead they are likely to "integrate" everyone's interests by ignoring their own. As Bill Puka argues, even at the

third stage of care, women are likely to acknowledge only their unthreatening interests. They will "ferret out spheres of power for pursuing these interests within the gaps of the established power structure" (Puka 1990, 66). The established power structure, or that which carers accept as given, is the relationship itself. Thus the ethic of care undermines a carer's autonomy.

Now I will turn to Gilligan's second response to the argument that an overriding emphasis on sustaining one's relationships undermines a carer's autonomy. This response is in effect to accept this argument and to de-emphasize sustaining one's relationships. That is, although Gilligan holds that the third stage of care allows one to dissipate tensions between self and other, she also holds that the third stage entails the recognition that moral problems make it *inevitable* that someone will be hurt. For instance, she writes that "although the conflict between self and other remains, the moral problem is restructured in an awareness that the occurrence of the dilemma itself precludes non-violent resolution" (Gilligan 1986a, 331). For example, a woman at the third level recognizes that her pregnancy is itself a result of the failure to care for both self and other, and that she must now choose between "hurting herself or ending the incipient life of the child" (Gilligan 1986a, 329). Although she recognizes that the dilemma does not allow for an inclusive solution, she also recognizes that it provides her an opportunity to "take control of her life," a process she begins by ending the self-destructive relationship which resulted in the pregnancy (Gilligan 1986a, 331). She tries to minimize hurt by doing so "in a decent, human kind of way . . . one that leaves maybe a slightly shaken but not totally destroyed person" (Gilligan 1982, 95). This woman exemplifies the highest stage of care, and there is little question that she also demonstrates autonomy. She critically evaluates her relationship with her lover and with the child that she might have, and in both cases decides that it is more responsible to end than to continue these relationships.

This response represents a challenge to the ideal type of the ethic of care, according to which it cannot be caring to end a relationship. In fact, the view that sustaining one's relationships is the top priority of an ethic of care is based on faulty reasoning. It is based on a conflation of a relational ontology with a relational ethics. Gilligan emphasizes that the ethic of care is grounded in a relational ontology. She claims that the care orientation's focus on sustaining one's relationships grows out of its recognition of our social situatedness. But accepting that one is ontologically socially situated does not commit one to sustaining one's relationships. Even if we reject all relationships to others, we will still be socially situated ontologically. The fact that one is socially constituted does not impose any moral obligations on us, and the claim that it does is a form of the naturalistic fallacy.

Perhaps the ethic of care relies on a *psychological* rather than a *logical* connection here. Gilligan has shown that there is a psychological connection between recognizing one's relatedness and believing that one should sustain one's relationships. Because women tend to *experience* themselves as connected to others, they

tend to focus on maintaining their social relationships. Perhaps those who recognize that they are socially situated cannot feel fulfilled unless they are socially connected to others. However, even if we understand this connection psychologically, it does not follow that in order to be fulfilled we have to maintain the relationships we are now in. The relationships we are now in may not be fulfilling at all, but instead may be destructive. Although caring relationships may be necessary to our survival, it does not follow that we need to be in any *particular* caring relations. Thus in its overriding emphasis on maintaining one's relationships, the ideal type of the ethic of care makes the mistake of taking a relational ontology to mean more than it does.

In fact, the recognition of the extent to which we are constituted by our relationships with others should lead us to be especially careful about the relationships we maintain, as the health of our relationships is not separable from our individual health. Moreover, sometimes caring for the other person's well-being can lead us to break off an unhealthy relationship with that person. Although by definition the ethic of care must make relationships its priority, it need not do so without regard for the quality of those relationships. Perhaps the fundamental priority of the ethic of care should be understood as a commitment to *healthy* caring relationships. One of the criteria for healthy caring relationships is that they allow for the autonomy of their members. Some of Gilligan's descriptions of the third level of care make it seem as if this is her intention. She refers to "an increasing differentiation of self and other" at the third level (Gilligan 1982, 74) and to "the possibility of a new kind of action that leaves both self and other intact" (Gilligan 1986a, 332). She suggests that at the third level, carers recognize that their identity is not completely bound up with their relationships. If a relationship does not allow them to retain that identity, then they are justified in ending it. Insofar as its priority is healthy relationships rather than relationships as such, the ethic of care allows for and promotes autonomy rather than undermining it.

It might be objected that this conclusion has saved the ethic of care only by prioritizing the ethic of justice, and its favored concept of autonomy, to the ethic of care. I think it is true that the ethic of care cannot be said to yield its *own* conception of autonomy, as Gilligan at times seems to suggest. However, as I showed in the first section of this chapter, a complete account of autonomy is not based solely in the ethic of justice, but is informed by both ethics. In particular, the ethic of care's attention to our social embeddedness reveals the ways in which an individual's self-determination is not separable from his or her relationships to others, both personal and more broadly social. The concept of autonomy defended here is one which would not result from either ethic by itself, but which emerges from the interaction of the two ethics. Moreover, using justice considerations in evaluating the ethic of care does not necessarily prioritize the ethic of justice; for, as I will show in the following chapters, we should also use care considerations in evaluating the ethic of justice.

In this section I have examined the relationship between care and autonomy from the perspective of the ethic of care and its relational ontology. I have shown that the ideal type of the ethic of care threatens the carer's autonomy by having the maintenance of one's relationships as its overriding priority. Following some of Carol Gilligan's work, I have suggested that the ethic of care might instead promote the carer's autonomy by prioritizing creating and maintaining *healthy* relationships.

Conclusion

Each of the two approaches we have considered here has revealed important aspects of the relationship between care and autonomy, yet each of them is also limited by its extreme view of the self. The individualistic approach demonstrates the ways in which genuine care requires separation between individuals. For instance, care is distorted when the carer identifies so completely with the recipient of care that she loses her critical perspective. Care is also distorted when it denies the recipient's individual identity. However, in the attempt to protect individual identities, the individualistic approach overlooks the senses in which care requires connection between individuals. For example, it draws sharp distinctions between different individuals' well-beings, when central to the care orientation is the recognition that the well-beings of self and other are linked. Similarly, the tendency to understand relationships on a contractual model neglects the fact that our caring relationships are often not chosen, but simply given.

In contrast, the emphasis on the social construction of identity that typically accompanies the ethic of care is helpful in allowing us to recognize the ways in which genuine care requires connection between individuals. It is also valuable because it shows the ways in which inclusive solutions allow one to preserve one's autonomy when fair solutions might not. However, when the social constitution of the self is interpreted to mean that one has an overriding obligation to preserve one's relationships, it undermines the carer's autonomy. The carer's autonomy is also undermined when she believes that she and the other are so connected that their well-beings are inseparable, when in fact they are to some degree distinct.

Thus it is the ideal types of the ethic of justice and the ethic of care that have given rise to the commonly held view that care and autonomy are necessarily incompatible. That is, the individualism of the ideal type of the ethic of justice is incompatible with care, while the social emphasis of the ideal type of the ethic of care is incompatible with autonomy. Therefore, reconciling care and autonomy requires moving beyond these ideal types and finding the right balance between the connections and separations between individuals. A number of commentators have searched for terminology to express this balance. For instance, Elizabeth Frazer and Nicola Lacey write:

The notion of the relational self, in contrast to both atomistic and inter-subjective selves, nicely captures our empirical and logical interdependence and the centrality to our identity of our relations with others and with practices and institutions, whilst retaining an idea of human uniqueness and discreteness as central to our sense of ourselves. It entails the collapse of any self/other or individual/community dichotomy without abandoning the idea of genuine agency and subjectivity. (Frazer and Lacey 1993, 178)

We need a concept like the relational self described here in order to overcome the standard dichotomy between care and autonomy.

In this chapter we have established the connection between ideal care and autonomy, while acknowledging that conventional care often undermines autonomy. This leaves us the project of challenging the barriers between conventional care and ideal care. I will turn to this in the next chapter.

Notes

1. Some moral philosophers in the Kantian tradition make a third requirement for autonomy, namely that one make moral decisions from an *impartial* perspective. In this view decisions based on "the special feelings that stem from particular personal relationships" are not autonomous (Hill 1989, 92). It is easy to see how this version of autonomy might conflict with an ethic of care, which is usually understood as a partialist ethic arising out of personal relationships. But I will not accept this requirement for autonomy. Kant held that autonomy requires impartiality because he believed that the true self is one free from all particular features; it is a self that all moral agents share. Thus, for Kant, acting based on one's true self requires acting impartially. But there is no reason to accept this conception of autonomy if we maintain that one's individuating features play a part in constituting one's true self, and I believe that they do. Autonomy need not require impartiality. Thus an ethic of care can be a partialist ethic without thereby ruling out autonomy.

2. See Meyers (1989) Part 2, Section 1.

3. See Meyers (1989) Part 2, Section 2.

4. See, for example, Christman (1989).

5. I will come back to this point in Chapter 6.

6. This is one aspect of the ethic of care's contextuality.

7. Of course, there remains a tension based on who decides what constitutes care, the carer or the recipient of care, but this isn't a tension that can be explained away.

8. This approach is also seen in Mary Parker Follett's "integrative" solutions, discussed in Mansbridge (1991a).

◢ 3 ◣

Care and Autonomy in Practice

▼

Feminist discussions of the ethic of care tend to commit one of two errors. Those which champion the ethic often abstract it from its social context, so that questions about the normative merits of the ethic of care become separate from questions about the role of that ethic in women's oppression. Carrie Menkel-Meadow exemplifies this approach when she writes: "I think it is useful to ask—even if one's sense of care and of relationship has developed out of the necessity for survival in the world in which one has been powerless—if those values are intrinsically important" (DuBois et al. 1985, 57). While the intrinsic importance of the ethic of care is a necessary condition for any defense of it, it is far from a sufficient condition. Similarly, Nel Noddings responds to Barbara Houston's worries about whether an ethic of care can avoid self-sacrifice by insisting that care should be understood as an ethic for everyone, not just women. She adds that the ethic of care's relational ontology means that caring for others amounts to caring for oneself, so that the ethic in some sense precludes the possibility of self-sacrifice (Noddings 1990a, 172–3). This tendency to celebrate the ethic of care by abstracting from the real connections between care and women's powerlessness is likely to reinforce those connections.

A second error occurs in the work of those who most vigorously attack the ethic of care. These critics are often so focused on the social context of care that they view questions about its intrinsic value as not just naive but pernicious. From this perspective the ethic of care is nothing more than women's expression of powerlessness. For instance, Catherine MacKinnon calls Gilligan's "different voice" the "voice of the victim speaking without consciousness" (DuBois et al. 1985, 27). She argues that Gilligan is mistaken to accept the words of her twelve-year-old respondent, Amy, as representing her own voice. Amy cannot use her own voice, according to MacKinnon, because there is a male "foot on her throat" (DuBois et al. 1985, 75). While an attention to power issues is crucial, it is a mistake to *reduce* discussions of care to power issues. By interpreting all relationships as hierarchical, this approach misses the insight of those who espouse the care orientation that relationships, even those between men and women, can have nonhierarchical dimensions. That is, attaining equal power to others is not the only important value; closeness to others is also important. A responsible discussion of the ethic of care must avoid both of these errors: It must pay attention to the social context of care without equating what the ethic of care says with the distorted ways it is often practiced.

My last chapter was addressed to critics of the ethic of care who make the mistake of reducing care to its often distorted practices. The seemingly pervasive tensions we see between care and autonomy lead such critics to conclude that care and autonomy are necessarily mutually exclusive. Against this view I showed that ideal care—defined as care which most benefits its recipient—not only allows for, but in many cases *requires* an autonomous caregiver. The theoretical compatibility of autonomy and care is evidence that their practical conflicts are merely contingent.

Until we address the very real practical tensions between autonomy and care, however, their theoretical compatibility will not have much meaning. I will open this chapter by examining several situations in which care and autonomy seem to conflict, and will show that these conflicts arise for different reasons, some more important than others. Some conflicts, while real, are isolated instances running contrary to general patterns. Other conflicts are the result of symbolic and institutional structures that construct care and autonomy in opposition to each other. These structures, I will argue, are the fundamental reasons for the pervasive tensions between care and autonomy, and thus I will devote the remainder of the chapter to examining the symbolism and the institutionalization of care.

There are a number of apparent exceptions to the claim that ideal care requires an autonomous caregiver. I have defined autonomy as requiring the capacity for critical thought, and, depending on how one interprets "critical" thought, this might seem an excessive requirement in many cases. For instance, simple caring acts in cases of obvious need do not seem to require a capacity for critical thought. One need not be especially autonomous to offer food to a hungry person. I acknowledge that there are instances in which a caregiver need not be autonomous to offer ideal care, but I contend that these are isolated instances. Ordinarily, caregiving takes place *over time* and as a result presents situations which require a critical capacity. Even a caregiver whose tasks are carefully defined by her superiors will sometimes face situations in which normal expectations break down and she must exercise her own critical capacity. Although offering a hungry person food on one occasion does not necessarily require critical thinking skills, doing what would most help this person—for example, challenging the social structures that allow people to go hungry—does require these skills. So, while there may be situations in which ideal care does not require a caregiver's autonomy, these situations are exceptions to the norm. Determining what *most* benefits someone typically requires taking a critical perspective.

I will now turn to a second group of exceptions to my strong claims about the relationship between care and autonomy. Sometimes a caregiver is mistaken about what is best for the recipient, and if she is allowed to act autonomously, she will hurt the recipient rather than help him. However, I do not claim that the caregiver's autonomy is a *guarantee* of ideal care. In other words, I do not hold that everyone's interests are always coincidental; there are situations in which what is best for the caregiver—autonomy—is not best for the recipient. Ideal care does not *necessarily* require an autonomous caregiver.

I do claim, however, that an autonomous caregiver is *more likely* to give ideal care than a nonautonomous one. Martin Benjamin and Joy Curtis make this point with regard to moral autonomy: "there is no guarantee that ethically autonomous actions are morally correct, but there is good reason to believe that free actions based on rational deliberation and moral reflection are more likely to be right than actions determined in other ways" (Benjamin and Curtis 1987, 404). This is because an autonomous caregiver is in the best position to assess what will most benefit the recipient. Promoting the recipient's well-being may require deferring to the judgment of others with more expertise on the recipient's well-being (including the recipient). But this is not inconsistent with the caregiver's autonomy; it is actually an expression of it. So while I do not deny that a caregiver may be autonomous but provide less than ideal care, I contend that in most circumstances care is threatened more by the caregiver's nonautonomy than by her autonomy.

A third kind of conflict between care and autonomy is the most important. These conflicts arise when the requirements of care work undermine the caregiver's autonomy. As caregiving work is typically defined, it does not require or even allow for the caregiver's critical thought, but is essentially the work of following the instructions of others—those of either the recipient of care or the "experts" for whom the caregiver works. Those with power over the caregiver define what counts as good care; the caregiver's own definition of good care is overridden, which means that the caregiver's autonomy is likewise overridden. Here the conflict is not the one just discussed between autonomy and ideal care, but between autonomy and care as it is socially defined. In theory, caregiving may typically require the caregiver's autonomy, but in practice, caregiving tends to preclude the caregiver's autonomy.

One way to respond to such cases is to argue that the care required of such a caregiver is not really "care." This was my tactic in the last chapter. It is also the tactic of feminists who distinguish between "caregiving" and "personal service." According to this distinction, caregiving is characterized by reciprocity between the caregiver and the recipient of care and by caring motivation, while personal service is characterized by the recipient's power over the caregiver and the caregiver's purely instrumental motivation. Emily Abel and Margaret Nelson write:

Those who provide personal services are members of subordinate groups in society who operate from a desire to please others and win their approval; they cannot anticipate receiving equivalent aid in return. Caregiving, by contrast, is rooted in reciprocity. Caregivers of children have once been young, caregivers of the infirm expect others to care for them when they are in need. Unlike providers of personal service, caregivers are motivated primarily by a concern for the well-being of those they tend. (Abel and Nelson 1990, 6–7)

This distinction between caregiving and personal service could allow us to take the view that care and autonomy are strongly compatible, even in practice. While distorted care, or personal service, may threaten the caregiver's autonomy, true care cannot do so. Caregivers autonomously seek to promote the well-being of the recipient of care. However, providers of personal service are not autonomous, but neither are they caregivers, so they do not represent a threat to the claim that care and autonomy are compatible.

However, in a discussion of the practical relationship between care and autonomy, it would be a mistake to make much of this distinction between caregiving and personal service. First, it would make the claim of compatibility between care and autonomy empty by defining care so that it *cannot* conflict with autonomy. Many activities normally considered caregiving would be disregarded because technically they fell in the category of personal service. But second and more importantly, the distinction between caregiving and personal services cannot be neatly drawn in practice. Even the most paradigmatic instances of caregiving often include aspects of personal service. For instance, even the best nurses are not motivated *solely* by concern for their patients. As Abel and Nelson write,

In practice, caregiving often cannot be disentangled from personal service. In a society riven by divisions of class, race, and gender, relationships of mutuality are difficult to achieve. In both the domestic domain and the waged labor force, most caregivers are members of subordinate groups, who provide care from compulsion and obligation as well as warmth and concern. (Abel and Nelson 1990, 7)

In this chapter, I will not try to reconcile the tensions between care and autonomy by distinguishing between caregiving and personal service, or between what I have called ideal care and distorted care.

The practical tensions between care and autonomy cannot be explained away as isolated instances. In our society, being a caregiver often means sacrificing one's autonomy. In the rest of this chapter, I will take a first step toward reconciling care and autonomy by identifying the sources of these tensions. I will show that the pervasive conflicts between care and autonomy are the result of a number of symbolic and institutional structures that put care and autonomy in conflict in our society.

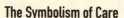

The Symbolism of Care

In this section I will explore the symbolic conflicts between care and auton-omy. First, I should indicate what I mean by "symbolic" conflicts. Some con-cepts are *defined* in opposition to one another, and thus *necessarily* conflict, such as lying and truth-telling. The conflict between care and autonomy is not of this kind. These concepts do not *necessarily* conflict, but it is neverthe-less difficult to be both caring and autonomous in our society because care and autonomy are socially constructed in opposition to one another. Indeed, care is socially constructed as feminine, autonomy is socially constructed as masculine, and the feminine and the masculine are socially constructed in opposition to one another. But to understand the force of this opposition between masculinity and femininity, we will have to see how this opposition fits into a broader symbolic system. Carol Gilligan summarizes this system as follows:

> The qualities deemed necessary for adulthood—the capacity for autonomous think-ing, clear decision making, and responsible action—are those associated with mas-culinity but considered undesirable as attributes of the feminine self. The stereotypes suggest a splitting of love and work that relegates the expressive capac-ities requisite for the former to women while the instrumental abilities necessary for the latter reside in the masculine domain. (Gilligan 1986a, 310)

In what follows I will show how the symbolic system that dichotomizes public and private, masculinity and femininity, work and love, and instrumentality and expressivity results in a dichotomy between care and autonomy.

The Femininity of Care

First, I need to address a set of criticisms that have arisen concerning women's use of the ethic of care. Doing so should clarify what I mean by the symbolic femi-ninity of care and show why I think it is important. Gilligan herself seems ambivalent about what kind of correlation she wants to claim between the ethic of care and femininity. At times she asserts that there is a strong empirical corre-lation between women and the ethic of care, while at others she insists that the ethic of care is characterized not by gender, but by theme. As Susan Moller Okin writes:

> A problem arises from the fact that it is not clear to what extent Gilligan is assert-ing generalizations about men's and women's moral thinking. Throughout most of the book, the language implies that strong general statements are being made about "men" and "women." By comparison, in the introduction, Gilligan mini-mizes her intent to generalize about gender differences in moral thinking. (Okin 1990, 156)

Gilligan's imprecision about whether and in what sense care is feminine has given rise to a great deal of debate over Gilligan's intentions and her success in carrying them out.

A number of critics have charged that Gilligan has not succeeded in showing an empirical connection between women and the ethic of care, but has merely articulated and defended the virtues we associate with women. Catherine Greeno and Eleanor Maccoby argue that Gilligan's work comes dangerously close to buying into our traditional stereotypes of men and women. They write:

> We can only sound a warning: women have been trapped for generations by people's willingness to accept their own intuitions about the truth of gender stereotypes. To us, there seems no alternative to the slow, painful, and sometimes dull accumulation of quantitative data to show whether the infinite variations in the way human beings think, feel, and act are actually linked to gender. (Greeno and Maccoby 1986, 315–316)

According to such critics, then, the femininity of the ethic of care is an empirical matter; the feminine and the female are identical. As Diane Romain writes, "Isn't it time we stopped classifying characteristics as feminine or masculine when we have no evidence that all and only females or males have such characteristics?" (Romain 1992, 35) These critics charge that if Gilligan cannot provide *empirical* proof that women use the ethic of care, her work merely perpetuates damaging stereotypes.

On the other extreme, Joan Tronto argues that "the debate around the ethic of care should be centered not in discussions of gender difference but in discourse about the ethic's adequacy as a moral theory" (Tronto 1987, 646). From this perspective, even if there were a strong empirical correlation between women and the ethic of care, it would be a mistake to label care a feminine ethic. First of all, questions about women's use of the ethic are irrelevant to the ethic's worth. Joan Williams writes, "To the extent that this claim [that women are focused on relationships while men are not] pinpoints actual gender differences, I argue it merely reflects the oppressive realities of the current gender system" (Williams 1989, 802). Although women may be more likely to adopt the ethic of care, this empirical fact is irrelevant to whether or not they *ought* to do so. Moreover, given a social context in which the masculine is considered normal, labeling the ethic feminine is in effect to label it inferior. According to these critics, advocates of the ethic of care can hope to make their case only by presenting the ethic in a de-gendered form and defending it based on its intrinsic value. I followed this course in the last chapter by arguing that care and autonomy need not come into conflict, but are actually mutually supportive concepts. However, while this argument is necessary to a defense of the ethic of care, it is not sufficient because in practice care and autonomy *do* come into conflict, and unless we can overcome these conflicts, the theoretical compatibility of care and autonomy will be irrelevant.

I suggest that Gilligan's ambivalence as well as much of the debate over the femininity of care arises from an acceptance of a false dichotomy: There is either a strong empirical correlation between women and the ethic of care *or* there is no special connection between femininity and the ethic of care. In fact, even if there is no strong empirical correlation between women and care, there is a strong *symbolic* connection between femininity and the ethic of care. As Jane Mansbridge writes, "While statistically there might be only a small difference between males and females in adherence to an ethic of care, culturally an ethic of care is female" (Mansbridge 1991b, 13–14). The ethic of care is symbolically feminine in the sense that we tend to associate its values with women, just as we tend to associate the values of the ethic of justice with men. As Marilyn Friedman puts it, the genders are moralized: "Moral norms about appropriate conduct, characteristic virtues and typical vices are incorporated into our conceptions of femininity and masculinity, female and male" (Friedman 1987a, 89). While Gilligan may not have shown that women really use the ethic of care, she has certainly articulated the ethic that is culturally associated with them.

Moreover, the fact that *In a Different Voice* has been received enthusiastically by so many women indicates that many women do identify with and seek validation for this ethic. Thus Friedman holds that the symbolically female voice Gilligan discerns is "more a matter of how we *think* we reason than of how we actually reason" (Friedman 1987a, 96). As Mansbridge explains, because gender is such a salient category, gender-coded characteristics become especially important in individuals' self-images. "If people learn that certain features of their own being are socially salient, they will notice those features more than others. This process exaggerates the importance of these features, as they become parts of a self-image" (Mansbridge, 1991b, 7). As a result, studies which attempt to compare male and female moral orientations get differing results depending on whether the subjects know what is being measured. For instance, while women and men do not differ significantly in studies measuring helping behavior, they differ greatly in studies which ask them to measure their own empathy. Empathy is socially coded as feminine in the United States, and subjects respond accordingly: Women are likely to report that they are empathetic, while men are likely to report that they are not (Mansbridge 1991b).

Greeno and Maccoby would no doubt respond that if the connection between the ethic of care and women is more symbolic than behavioral, we are dealing in stereotypes rather than realities. In doing so, they would argue, we reinforce these stereotypes. But to recognize and discuss stereotypes is not necessarily to accept them. Although many women do not use an ethic of care, stereotypes and realities are not entirely distinct. First, realities help create stereotypes: A stereotype may take root because of relatively noticeable differences at one time, and persist when those differences have greatly diminished at a later time. Stereotypes also help create realities. Because our experiences are largely shaped by cultural myths about gender, and because our moral orientations largely arise out of our experiences, it would be surprising if some differences did not arise between the moral orientations of men and women. Even if these differences were only minuscule, however, we could not understand the conflicts between care and autonomy if we ignored the traditional symbolic femininity of care. If we are concerned about changing the social conditions that dichotomize care and autonomy, we must focus on and challenge the sources of the stereotypes that help create those conditions.

The Care/Work Dichotomy

Although care and autonomy are mutually compatible in theory, the symbolic conflicts between them run deep. These conflicts are part of the broader opposition between feminine-coded concepts linked to the private sphere and masculine-coded concepts linked to the public sphere. Our ideology of separate sexual spheres reached what we now consider its "traditional" form in the nineteenth century. Until then, many households in Western Europe and the United States were economic units as well as a familial units. While male and female roles were far from identical, both men and women had responsibilities for production as well as family care. With the Industrial Revolution, however, the household ceased to be a production unit, so that family relations and production were separated and the gender division of labor was intensified. Men worked outside of the home for pay, while women worked inside the home tending to the well-being of family members, and were economically dependent on their husbands. Of course this was not true of all men, women, or families, but it was increasingly common and most important, increasingly a cultural ideal. The separation between the feminine private sphere and the masculine public sphere took on its modern form as natural and inevitable. Francesca Cancian writes,

> As the daily activities of men and women grew further apart, a new world view emerged that exaggerated the differences between the personal, loving, feminine sphere of the home and the impersonal, powerful, masculine sphere of the workplace. (Cancian 1986, 697)

In what follows I will explore some of the differences that this world view has exaggerated, and show that this world view is ultimately responsible for the conflicts between care and autonomy.

One difference that this view exaggerates is the difference between work done in the home and outside the home. Since the nineteenth century, work in the home has taken on a new character. Since much domestic labor has been altered by technology, there has been an increased emphasis on the emotional aspects of taking care of a family. Men's work outside the home is paid, usually has a regular schedule, and produces goods or services for exchange on a market, while traditionally, women's work in the home is none of these things (McDowell and

Pringle 1992, 122). But cultural processes have exaggerated these differences by taking men's work as paradigmatic and defining "work" itself only in terms of the features of male work. As a result, women's caregiving activities in the home have come to be considered nonwork, introducing a dichotomy between home and work: "Work is often experienced as the opposite of home; it constitutes the "public" side of our everyday life, as distinct from the more "private" or intimate side shared with family and friends" (McDowell and Pringle 1992, 122). Women's caregiving in the home has come to be considered not just a different kind of work than men's work, but the *opposite* of work.

This dichotomy between home and work is associated with the common view of care as a feeling. As Hilary Graham writes, "Everyday conversations about caring are generally recognized to be conversations about feelings. When we talk about 'caring' for someone, we are talking about our emotions" (Graham 1983, 15). Thus the activities involved in caregiving are seen as secondary to the emotions that give rise to those activities. Rosemary Pringle describes the emotionalization of housework as follows:

> Laundering was not just laundering but an expression of love .... Cleaning the bathroom sink was not just cleaning, but an exercise of protective maternal instincts, providing a way for the housewife to keep family free from disease. (Pringle 1992, 151)

While care is interpreted as emotional responsiveness based on affection for others, work is interpreted as activity undertaken for its instrumental benefits. Care is an expression of one's identity, while work is a mere transaction of goods and services. Care allows us to connect with others, while work is generally unpleasant and burdensome. When the contrasts between care and work are drawn in this way, it seems as if one would degrade care by labeling it work (DeVault 1991, 229–230). Care is something more meaningful than mere work.

I want to argue that this dichotomy between care and work depends on unacceptably narrow concepts of both care and work. First, caring is not limited to or reducible to feelings; it requires caregiving activities as well. As Cancian writes,

> In reality, a major way by which women are loving is in the clearly instrumental activities associated with caring for others, such as preparing meals, washing clothes, and providing care during illness. (DeVault 1991, 229–230)

Although caregiving work is generally an expression of emotional closeness, this is not always the case. As I noted earlier, in many cases caregiving is motivated not solely by affection for the recipient of care, but by some form of compulsion as well. Graham writes, "Caring is experienced as a labour of love in which the labour must continue even when the love falters" (Graham 1983, 16). (It is also true that conventional work is not always simply instrumentally motivated, but often has intrinsic rewards as well.) By focusing exclusively on the emotional dimensions of care and ignoring its instrumental and active dimensions, we exaggerate the differences between care and other work.

But it is a mistake to label even the emotional dimensions of care nonwork. It is often thought that we choose our actions, but that our feelings are simply given. If this were so we could have no control over our feelings, and therefore we could not be obligated to have any particular feelings. In fact, however, we do have some control over our emotions. As Arlie Hochschild has shown, we often "manage" our feelings according to individual and social expectations (Hochschild 1983). Although we cannot simply choose to feel a particular way, we can, in Aristotelian fashion, choose to engage in those activities that will help us develop the kinds of feelings that we would like to have. To the degree that we have this kind of control over our feelings, we can be held responsible for them. As Michael Stocker notes, "we do criticize ourselves and others for not having or showing proper affection. For instance, parents are criticizable if they do not have and express love for their children" (Stocker 1987, 65–66). Thus even the emotional aspects of the ethic of care involve work. Although the efforts involved in developing the appropriate feelings are not what we typically think of as work, they indicate that we need a broader understanding of work.

The view of care as fundamentally about uncontrolled and uncontrollable feelings has a number of undesirable consequences. It contributes to the dichotomy between care and autonomy by suggesting that while we are either autonomous or nonautonomous with regard to our actions, questions about the autonomy of care are misplaced. It also plays into the conception of women as "naturally" caring. If caring is a natural expression of women's personality, then questions about the just distribution of caregiving responsibilities do not arise. Men, or those for whom care is not "natural," cannot be expected to be caring. However, women can be expected to be caring, and, since they are simply expressing themselves, need not be given special credit for their care. Marjorie DeVault writes:

> The association of caring with women's personality suggests that caring comes naturally for women, and the idea that women's "caring for" should be taken as evidence of love produces compelling social pressure to do the work, especially within families. Both of these ideas serve prevailing arrangements that depend on women's caring work without explicitly recognizing needs for care. (DeVault 1991, 239–240)

So far I have focused on two reasons care should be recognized as work: First, the differences between caregiving and other kinds of work have been exaggerated, and second, managing our emotions requires a kind of work that we usually fail to recognize. But as DeVault points out, the underlying reason we should recognize care as work is that doing so reflects an explicit recognition of its social importance.

Care is not considered work because its social value is not recognized. Work is an honorific label for activities that those with public, powerful voices take seriously as socially necessary (DeVault 1991). Thus the contributions of subordinate members of society are likely to be considered nonwork, or at most unskilled work. In particular, work coded as feminine is considered menial, trivial, or easy. Housewives frequently describe themselves as "just housewives" who "stay home" rather than "work at home." Kathryn Morgan writes of a woman in her early fifties who in describing herself said that she had "raised seven children and then went back to work" (Morgan 1987, 221). These attitudes apply whether the work is private unpaid work, or public paid work. Hilary Rose writes:

> Within public caring labour the relational skills of women, even where acknowledged, as when it is said that a patient needs TLC, still do not rate acknowledgment in terms of status or financial reward. In the domestic context women's nurturative qualities are simultaneously praised and seen as pre-scientific practices awaiting the emancipatory certainty of scientific knowledge. (Rose 1986, 165)

The esteem in which a particular kind of work is held influences the degree of autonomy a worker is given in the way he does his work. Those who do work that is considered important and difficult are thought to require and deserve some control over the way they do that work. Yet those who do work that is considered menial, trivial, or easy are thought to neither need nor deserve such control. In short, because the work label reflects the esteem in which an activity is held, the dichotomy between care and work sets up a dichotomy between care and autonomy. Later in the chapter I will explore various kinds of care work to show the ways it compromises the autonomy of its workers.

Before I do so, however, I need to address a criticism of my argument in this section. I have suggested that by recognizing care as work we will help improve its status. But it might be argued that in our culture, *most* work compromises the autonomy of workers. That is, it should come as no surprise that when care is considered work it compromises the autonomy of care workers; this is merely part of the general problem of the alienation of labor. Thus by labeling care as work we may actually be *lowering* its status. Perhaps we should resist labeling care as work on the grounds that while work is typically unpleasant and burdensome, care is something more meaningful.

The view that care is not work because it is something better than work has some relation to the view that women are not equal to men because they are *better* than men. Both constructions serve not only to ennoble women but also to reinforce their subordination. Caregiving may be an especially noble type of work, but if so, this is *despite* rather than *because* we refuse to acknowledge the effort it involves by calling it work. Most of the ways Americans treat care workers reveal that we do not hold them in high esteem.

Moreover, while the conflicts between care work and autonomy are in some ways similar to the conflicts between other kinds of work and autonomy, they are in some ways unique. Because of the symbolic system I have explored in this section, care work compromises the worker's autonomy in a unique way, and thus deserves special treatment. Masculinity, the public sphere, instrumentality, work, and autonomy have been defined in opposition to femininity, the private sphere, emotional expressiveness, care, and subordination. Although there is nothing natural or inevitable about these dichotomies, they are important in organizing our thinking and influencing our actions. Although many kinds of work compromise workers' autonomy, the fact that care is coded as feminine while autonomy is coded as masculine introduces an additional conflict between care work and autonomy. Thus while we need to dismantle the whole symbolic system that gives rise to these dichotomies, broadening our conception of work to include caregiving is an important step in narrowing the tensions between care and autonomy. In the next section I will expand on this claim by showing specific ways in which care work presents special obstacles to the autonomy of caregivers.

The Institutional Conflicts Between Care and Autonomy

Before I go further, I need to provide some sort of definition of "care work," and indicate how it differs from non-care work. It is not possible or desirable to give a list of necessary and sufficient conditions for what counts as care work. Some kinds of work are paradigmatic examples of care work, such as nursing or parenting young children. But a number of other kinds of work are more difficult to classify. A physician, a housekeeper, a flight attendant, or even a bureaucrat may be a care worker in some senses but not in others. Rather than providing a precise definition of care work which would lead us to ignore the care work involved in these diverse kinds of work, I will identify several features typical of care work.

First, care work typically takes place in the context of a personal relationship between caregiver and recipient. Second, the care worker acts to promote the well-being of others. Finally, the care worker is typically motivated in her work by a feeling of concern for the recipients of care (even if other motives, such as money, lead one to do the work in the first place). The more of these features that a kind of work involves, the more it qualifies as care work. But there is no sharp distinction between care work and non-care work.

Each of these three features of care work is socially interpreted in the United States today in a way that compromises the autonomy of care workers. I will briefly and generally show how this is so. First, the care worker's personal relationship to her clients allows her to know them as individuals rather than as abstractions, and thus to provide better care for them. The recognition that knowledge comes through direct contact is one of the most important insights of the ethic of care. Yet the particularity of care work is not generally recognized as a valuable source of knowledge but tends to be considered evidence that care work is less important work. In other words, care work's focus on the individual is interpreted in terms of the dichotomy between universality and particularity, according to which knowledge concerns general truths rather than particular details. As a result, the expertise care workers gain through their close contact with clients usually goes unrecognized, and generalists at a distance from the recipients of care are considered the experts of caregiving. The role of personal contact in care work is then used to justify denying caregivers autonomy over their work.

The second feature of care work threatens the worker's autonomy because of the interpretation socially given to the "well-being" of others that the care worker promotes. In Chapter 2, I defined ideal care as that which most benefits the recipient. Since the recipient may be mistaken about what will most benefit him or her, I argued that the caregiver needs to be autonomous to be able to provide the best care. In practice, however, care is defined not by an objective standard but by those with power over the caregiver. As a result, care work is typically defined as the work of following the instructions of others—instructions of either the recipient of care or the "experts" for whom the caregiver works. As I will show in my discussions of housework and nursing, care workers are expected to defer to others' judgments about the nature of the care they provide. In this sense they are expected to renounce their autonomy.

This renunciation might not seem to distinguish care work from most kinds of work. Most workers do not have the freedom to set the standards of their work. Most work requires some renunciation of the worker's autonomy. But the threats to the care worker's autonomy are unique because of the care worker's motivations, or the third feature distinguishing care work. Typically, the care worker is motivated not just by extrinsic rewards, but by a moral commitment to helping others. Thus when she is required to follow instructions with which she disagrees, the care worker is not just forbidden to do what she *wants* to do. She is also forbidden to do what she believes she *ought* to do. A shoe salesman may disagree with his boss about the organization of the storeroom, and his views may be especially valuable because they are based on his personal experience of using the storeroom every day. When his boss overrules him he may be angry, and may feel that his sense of self as a creator and possessor of his work has been violated, but he is unlikely to feel that his *conscience* has been violated. In contrast, a teacher who disagrees with her principal about how to deal with a troubled student and whose views are overruled *is* likely to feel that her conscience has been violated. For this reason, threats to a care worker's autonomy are deeper and more personal than threats to the autonomy of most workers. Of course, the care worker could refuse to follow the judgment of her superior and follow the dictates of her own conscience, thus preserving her moral autonomy. However, asserting one's autonomy in this situation would threaten one's livelihood, and thus such a care worker cannot be said to be autonomous in the more broadly social sense.

In the rest of the chapter I will examine the institutional tensions between care work and autonomy in more detail. I will focus on two categories of care work: unpaid care work in family life and paid care work in caregiving institutions, specifically nursing. I will follow DeVault's convention of calling unpaid care work in family life housework, and the worker a houseworker. I have chosen these categories of care work for several reasons. First, they are the most common kinds of care work. No matter what occupation women have, most provide unpaid care work in family life or paid care work in employment institutions, or both. Second, these two categories illustrate threats to the caregivers' autonomy from opposite ends of the caregiving process. The houseworker's autonomy is usually threatened by the recipients of her care, while the nurse's autonomy is usually threatened by the bureaucracy in which she works. Finally, these categories of public and private caregiving allow me to focus not only on the tensions within each of these spheres but also on the tensions *between* these two spheres of work. This is important because the public/private dichotomy is in many ways responsible for the care/autonomy dichotomy.

Unpaid Care Work and Autonomy

The threats to the houseworker's autonomy are disguised by the fact that those who perform housework generally claim that they are autonomous, and reject the view that they are subservient (DeVault 1991). Housewives who discuss their work emphasize the degree of choice they have as compared to other kinds of workers. They point to the fact that they are to a large extent their own bosses, and, rather than following a routine set by an employer, they are in charge of the household routine and have a good deal of flexibility in deciding how to organize their work process. Houseworkers also report that compared to paid workers, who are generally expected to work hard no matter how they feel, they have more freedom to decide when to work hard and when not to. They also report that they have some freedom to avoid doing work they dislike (DeVault 1991, 159). Finally, rather than striving to meet standards established by others, houseworkers have a sense of setting their own standards. As Carol Pateman writes:

> The housewife is frequently presented as being in a very different position from a worker, a servant or a slave; a housewife is her own boss. Housewives see freedom from control as their great advantage; they stress that they can decide what to do and how and when to do it, and many housewives have strong internalized standards of what constitutes a good job of work. (Pateman 1988, 130)

In short, the expressed views of houseworkers themselves tend to count in favor of their autonomy.

However, despite all of the houseworker's freedoms in choosing how to carry out her work, the job of housework is (like many other kinds of work) ultimately a kind of service to others. The needs, preferences, and activities of other family members become givens around which the houseworker organizes her work. But typically she does not interpret her acceptance of the demands of others as compromising her own autonomy. Instead, recognizing the freedoms she has in organizing her work, the houseworker commonly interprets her deference to others' preferences as a fair compromise. Often she concludes that giving her own preferences the weight she gives other family members' preferences would be selfish. Moreover, making choices which would give equal weight to her own and others' preferences would make her work that much more difficult, so given her limited material resources and time, she chooses to defer to others. DeVault describes the reasoning she observed among houseworkers:

> The fact that so many women frame these accommodations as "choices" means that they are less likely to make choices more obviously on their own behalf when the interests of family members conflict. In such situations, women seem to assume that they have made enough choices, and often come to define deference as equity. (DeVault 1991, 160–1)

Paradoxically, then, houseworkers often reason that because they have the freedom to decide *how* to meet others' demands, it is only fair that they accept others' demands. In recognizing and appreciating the limited freedoms they enjoy in their work, houseworkers tend to overlook the fact that their work requires them to be subservient to their family.

It might seem unfair to challenge the degree of autonomy involved in housework when a houseworker herself claims that she is autonomous. After all, many women recognize that this work is both skilled and valuable, and take pride in doing it well. However, the underlying tensions between this kind of care work and autonomy surface when women choose *not* to favor others' interests over their own. Such women are often regarded—by other family members, and even by themselves—as uncaring and selfish. For such women, part of the work of housework comes to include concealing the effort it involves, so that caring seems like a natural expression of one's personality rather than work. In challenging her subordinate role, the houseworker reveals the effort involved in her caring, but the fact that her caring involves effort is itself interpreted as a flaw in her character. DeVault writes, "If the act of pressing a claim for time off, or help from others, is so fraught with interpersonal danger, it is perhaps not surprising that so many women choose to accommodate to inequitable arrangements instead of resisting them" (DeVault 1991, 156). Houseworkers see themselves as *choosing* to defer to others; however, given the conflict caused by choosing *not* to defer to others, deferring to others is often the best option consistent with the caring role of houseworker.

Thus unpaid care work in the family compromises the autonomy of the caregiver. Typically it does not involve blatant coercion, such as threats, but is more subtle and comes built into the role of houseworker and the expectations attached to the caregiving role itself. Nor is there any one person enforcing these expectations. Indeed, women in houseworker roles help enforce these expectations on themselves. Understanding why they do so requires recognizing the coercive effects of gender socialization which defines femininity in terms of self-sacrifice. Among the residual effects of such socialization, especially when one continues to live in such a gender-structured society, is a reduced ability to critically reflect on the gender roles one plays. One is unlikely to achieve autonomy when critical reflection on femininity violates one's own standards of femininity.

I have shown that the houseworker's interests are usually considered less important than the interests of other family members. But this differential power within the family in turn serves to undermine the autonomy of the unpaid caregiver even further. Specifically, women's roles as caregivers within the family serve to limit their paid work outside of the family, when it is through paid work that they could gain economic independence that could allow them more power within the family (Okin 1989a). Most women and their families regard women's role as primary caregivers within the family as a *given* which their paid work must accommodate. This means that women are often limited to part-time employment. But part-time employment is typically the lowest paid employment as well as the least likely to lead to advancement. Moreover, even when they work full-time in professional careers, women often feel limited in the commitment they can give their careers by their commitments to their families. It is impossible to combine the 60–80 hour work weeks expected for advancement in many professions with full-time or even dedicated part-time caregiving work at home.

DeVault's study indicates that men generally do not experience this kind of conflict between family and work responsibilities. Men who limit their professional commitments in order to do significant amounts of care work at home usually do so out of choice rather than obligation. The different degrees of choice involved in unpaid care work are reflected in women's and men's attitudes toward cooking for the family. DeVault reports that typically, women pay close attention to family members' tastes in food, and evaluate the success of a meal by how well it pleased family members. When their own preferences conflict with those of others, they are likely to yield to others, not only because it would seem selfish to do otherwise, but because meeting their own preferences in addition to everyone else's preferences would make it more difficult to prepare the meal. In contrast, when men cook for the family, they often do not feel the same obligation to satisfy the tastes of others. DeVault reports that in evaluating their cooking, men are more likely to focus on their own creativity in preparing the meal than on the pleasure it did or did not bring to the individuals served (DeVault 1991).

Men are also more able than women to choose whether to sacrifice their careers to meet family responsibilities: "Women know that if they do not sacrifice, *no one* will, whereas men assume that if *they* do not, women will" (Williams 1989, 831). Thus women often "choose" to subordinate or abandon their careers for their families, a choice which not only affirms their identity as caregivers but makes economic sense since men typically earn more than women. Of course, men earn more than women in the first place in part because they do not have the family responsibilities that women have. As Clare Ungerson puts it, "The ideology of housework and women's place within it has a material impact on women's paid work which in turn serves to reinforce that very ideology" (Ungerson 1983a, 38). It is deceptive to say that women *choose* to sacrifice their careers in favor of their family responsibilities. Rather, women's (unchosen) role as primary caregivers in the family *dictates* that they sacrifice their careers in favor of their family responsibilities. The inequality of women's unpaid care work undermines their autonomy not only within but outside the family.

Paid Care Work and Autonomy

Many women enter paid work in the hopes of promoting their own autonomy. Indeed, paid care work has several features which would seem to allow for the caregiver's autonomy in ways that unpaid care work does not. First, the mere fact that work is paid helps promote the worker's economic self-sufficiency. As Bernice Fisher writes, "Work in the public realm offers an escape for women—a way to become a citizen, a person, a worker who controls her own labor power" (Fisher 1990, 109). Second, unlike the unpaid care worker, the paid care worker usually is not isolated. Paid care workers who find their working conditions unfair can talk with one another and join together to try to change those conditions in ways that houseworkers cannot. Third, paid care work has limits absent in unpaid care work. The work schedule and the expectations of the houseworker are virtually unlimited: She has no real time off, and she is typically expected to ensure that her family is happy. As DeVault writes, "Mothers are held responsible for producing wholesome and healthful families, and they are taught to believe that their husbands' and children's problems result from inadequate performance of household duties" (DeVault 1991, 136). But paid care work, with its well-defined work schedules and expectations, seems to protect the care worker from these intrusions upon her autonomy.

Women also seek paid care work as an opportunity to express their caring orientation. They derive satisfaction from developing personal relationships with their clients and from working within these relationships to promote their clients' well-being. In other words, many women hope that paid care work will allow them to affirm their identity as carers while retaining control over their own lives, or to *overcome* the tensions between care and autonomy. Susan Reverby writes of aspiring nursing students that they "did not seem to separate autonomy and altruism, but rather sought its linkage through training" (Reverby 1990, 139). As I will show, however, this strategy for reconciling care and autonomy generally fails.

The difference between care as it is defined by the caregivers themselves and care as it is defined by the bureaucracies which employ them is often significant, and it is the basis of the tensions between caregiving work and the caregivers' autonomy. The caregiver and her employer often have different priorities for this work, and because the caregiver's continued employment depends upon accepting her employer's priorities, her role as a carer often compromises her own autonomy.

For instance, caregivers generally regard close interaction with their clients as both personally rewarding and as essential to the success of their caregiving. A nurse who gets to know her patients becomes aware of their individual needs in a way she would not otherwise. She is more attuned to their medical conditions and thus often notices subtle changes that physicians miss because they tend to see their patients briefly and less often. Developing a personal relationship to patients also allows a nurse to make informed decisions about their treatment. It is not only the caregiver who regards this personal interaction as important: Patients also consider their personal relationships to their caregivers an essential part of the care they receive.

In contrast, health care institutions generally give a higher priority to other aspects of care, particularly the more strictly quantifiable aspects such as physical patient care and record keeping. These narrowly instrumental tasks often dominate caregivers' work to such an extent that they can find little time to give the emotional care that they consider so important. But because they do consider this care so important, and because the patients do as well, caregivers feel obligated to break their work rules in order to provide it. As Karen Sacks puts it, "the informal rules expect these workers to do what the formal rules prohibit" (Sacks 1990, 190). Not surprisingly, these conflicting demands take a toll on caregivers. They are willing to take low-status, low-paid work because, despite these drawbacks, it offers personal rewards. Yet they find out that even these rewards are largely denied. Abel and Nelson write:

> As personal commitment wanes, some workers seek other types of employment. Some of those who remain gradually assimilate to the bureaucratic mold and become emotionally detached from their clients. Despite the idealism and altruism that originally may have motivated them, they deliver a mechanistic form of care. (Abel and Nelson 1990, 16)

This shift in priorities from emotional care to strictly physical care perpetuates itself: the requirement that caregivers focus their energies on quantifiable, instrumental care results in high turnover rates among caregivers, which in turn hinders the development of personal relationships essential to more holistic care.

Why, then, do employers of caregivers give a higher priority to narrowly instrumental care over affective care? Bureaucracies must operate on the basis of general rules: "All of the problems that present themselves to the bureaucracy must become routine; that is, they must be standardized" (Fisher and Tronto 1990, 49). This means that patients cannot be treated as unique individuals but as instances of general types. Since caregiving requires attention to the individual in his or her uniqueness, there will always be tensions between bureaucracy and caregiving. These tensions have been exacerbated recently by cutbacks in public funding and by the movement toward for-profit health care services, both of which place even greater emphasis on efficiency (Fisher and Tronto 1990, 14). With higher productivity standards, the unquantifiable relational aspects of care become increasingly dispensable, so that when they exist it is despite rather than because of caregivers' work requirements.

Bureaucracy also undermines caregiving by its emphasis on specialization and hierarchization. Today a single patient is generally the joint responsibility of many different health care workers, each with his or her own focus and level of authority. While this division of labor often has medical benefits for the patient, it also has drawbacks. No single caregiver knows the patient personally and has the authority to make decisions about the patient's well-being. Those closest to the patient are the subordinate members of the health care team, and those with ultimate authority over the patient have little personal contact with the patient.

This points to a central problem in the practice of nursing. Traditionally, "the ethics of the nursing profession were essentially the ethics of obedience to physician's demands" (Kasachkoff 1987). As Sarah Dock, an early nursing leader, wrote in 1917, "Obedience is the first law and the very cornerstone of good nursing . . . she will never become a reliable nurse until she can obey without question" (Benjamin and Curtis 1987, 395). This delegation of authority is justified on the grounds that physicians have medical expertise that nurses lack, so that any disagreements the nurse might have with a physician's medical assessment need not be taken seriously. Thus, according to the traditional conception of nursing, a nurse fulfills her role of acting in the best interest of the patient by following physician's orders, even when she disagrees with those orders. In this traditional conception of nursing, caring and autonomy are incompatible. This is not just because nursing requires taking orders. Nurses are not literally coerced to carry out doctors' orders against their wills, but the fact that doing otherwise threatens their job security certainly disempowers them to some degree. More importantly, the institutionalization of the traditional conception of nursing has the effect of disabling nurses' critical judgment. When nurses are not rewarded but punished for thinking critically, they tend to leave the field or to adapt to the expectation that they simply follow orders.

This view of nursing presumes that obeying the physician will always promote the patient's well-being. Even though this may be true in most cases, it is clear that there are exceptions. Physicians, like all people, sometimes make obvious mistakes which they will immediately correct if they are made aware of them. It is not in the patient's best interest for the nurse to obey the physician in such cases. In other cases, a nurse has more expertise than a physician because of her personal knowledge of a patient or because of her extensive experience in a particular specialty. Such cases indicate that the nurse's obligation to obey physicians' orders should be understood as a prima facie duty rather than an absolute duty (Benjamin and Curtis 1987). The nurse's ultimate obligation is not to the physician but to her patients. Meeting this obligation to her patients not only allows for but requires her autonomy. The fact that a nurse is autonomous does not mean that she should never defer to the physician's judgment. Rather, it means that the physician-nurse relationship must be a collaborative rather than a strictly hierarchical one. Both parties should take the other's views seriously, and if possible, reach consensus about the patients' care. Obviously there are particular contexts, such as emergency situations, when it is impossible to seek a consensus and the physician's judgment must prevail, but these are the exceptions rather than the rule.

Even though there are good reasons that nursing should be autonomous, the traditional conception of nursing still prevails, challenged primarily by individual nurses who place themselves at personal risk by pursuing autonomy in their work. It is also challenged by nursing theorists who argue that nursing is a profession in its own right. They argue that nurses have their own areas of expertise which necessitate the collaborative practice of medicine with physicians. However, as it has developed, this movement toward professional status seems to require sacrificing the personal contact that identifies nursing as caregiving in the first place. Professional status is traditionally achieved through increasing formal, theoretical education and through specialization, but as nurses become specialized experts, others take over their personal interaction with patients. As Kari Waerness writes,

> This professionalization . . . implies that the least "glamorous" tasks must be sorted out and handed over to less skilled labour. It is not "efficient" that highly educated manpower should do things that can just as well be done by unskilled workers. (Waerness 1984a, 82)

Professionalizing nursing also seems to undermine caregiving by replacing personal attachments between nurses and patients with standardized techniques of "care" which can be instrumentally justified.

The lesson to be learned from these difficulties in reconciling autonomy and caregiving in nursing is not that nursing should not be professionalized, but rather that the institutional and symbolic tensions between care and autonomy are pervasive. That is, to be an autonomous worker, one must be a professional, but to be a professional, one must shed personalized caregiving tasks. Overcoming these tensions will require rethinking what it means to be a professional. The most effective nurse would be one who had not only extensive formal training but also extensive personal contact with patients (Noddings 1990a).

Conclusion

Overcoming the conflicts between care and autonomy will require fundamental social changes. As I have shown, the conflicts between care and autonomy are part of a symbolic system based on the fundamental dichotomy between public and private spheres. Thus challenging the care/autonomy dichotomy means challenging the public/private dichotomy. I will conclude this chapter by showing how achieving autonomous care would undermine the distinction between public values of justice and private values of care.

In paid care work, autonomous care would require, among other things, giving caregivers credit for the knowledge they gain through their close interaction with clients, and recognizing that the bureaucratic rules that typically govern caregiving institutions cannot do so adequately. This would challenge the traditional idea that the public sphere can and should be governed exclusively by universal rules. Applying these rules with a sensitivity to particulars requires valuing the particularistic ethic of care in public institutions where it is usually thought inappropriate (Ferguson 1984).

In unpaid care work, overcoming the conflict between care and autonomy would require redistributing power in the family. Rather than designating women as primary caregivers whether or not they work outside of the home, caregiving responsibilities would have to be justly distributed between men and women. Caring would be based on reciprocity rather than economic dependency. This redistribution would challenge the traditional conception of the private sphere as exclusively a realm of care. It would mean using the ethic of justice in family relations.

Moreover, if women and men shared caregiving responsibilities in the family, this sharing would require changes in all workplaces. Rather than assuming that the ideal worker has no caregiving responsibilities at home, employers would have to restructure their workplaces so that all workers could combine work and family responsibilities. By recognizing the connections between individuals' public and private lives, this would also challenge the public/private dichotomy.

In the next chapter I will challenge the public/private and care/justice dichotomies in the way I have suggested here. I will focus on questions about the possibility and the desirability of using an ethic of care in the public sphere.

4

Care, Justice, and the Public/Private Dichotomy

▼

Most moral philosophers maintain that the public and private spheres should operate according to different moral codes. Specifically, they maintain that the public sphere of government and civil society should be governed by abstract norms ensuring equality for all citizens, while the private sphere of family and personal relations should be governed by particularized norms oriented toward meeting individuals' needs.[1] In this view, the proper public morality is what I am calling the ethic of justice, and the proper private morality is what I am calling the ethic of care. I will call these boundaries of justice and care their *conventional boundaries*. A number of feminists have challenged the conventional boundaries of justice, and with the recent examination and defense of the ethic of care, the conventional boundaries of care have also come into question. Some advocates of the ethic of care have held that these boundaries implicitly devalue care, and have suggested that the ethic of care has important implications beyond the sphere of personal relations. In this chapter I will pursue this suggestion by critically examining the justifications offered for the conventional boundaries of care.

The ethic of care's two foremost defenders, Carol Gilligan and Nel Noddings, seem unsure about what position to take on its proper boundaries. Both of them defend an ethic that is at least modeled on personal relations, if not restricted to them, and have been vague and inconsistent about their views on the scope of the ethic of care. For instance, in her book *Caring*, Noddings defends caring not as a complement, but as an *alternative* to justice, thereby implying that she seeks to extend the boundaries of care to public contexts. Then again, she limits the scope of caring when she writes that because caring requires personal encounters with individuals, we cannot care for everyone. In response to recent critics, Noddings has acknowledged that she is "not ready to say exactly how justice and care should be combined" (Noddings 1990b, 120). For her part, Gilligan suggests that it would be not only possible but desirable to expand the boundaries of the ethic of care when she ends *In a Different Voice* with the assertion that human survival in the late twentieth century may depend more on an ethic of care than an ethic of justice.

▼

She does not expand, however, on this suggestion that the ethic of care be put to political use. In a later article, Gilligan writes that both the ethic of justice and the ethic of care must play a part in "public as well as private life" (Gilligan 1986c, 326). But, again, she has not specified what this might mean. So although both Noddings and Gilligan suggest that the ethic of care has applications beyond the sphere of personal relations, both seem hesitant to explore these applications.

There have been two kinds of critical reactions to this confusion over the appropriate boundaries of care. One group of critics considers the ethic of care *personal;* a second considers it *parochial.* The first criticism comes from those defending the conventional boundaries of justice and care. According to them, the ethic of care is and should be limited to personal relations, but this is not a problem, because the ethic of justice covers the ground outside these relations. For instance, in responding to Gilligan's work, Lawrence Kohlberg retreated from his early view that there is nothing distinctive about the ethic of care. He conceded that his theory of moral development tracks justice reasoning rather than moral reasoning as a whole. But he insisted that the ethic of care is not, as Gilligan suggests, a separate track of morality, but instead a moral approach suitable only for personal relationships. The ethic of care is unsuited to broader social and political relations; for these we must use the ethic of justice. Thus, according to Kohlberg, the ethic of care is valuable, but its specific range of application includes only our relationships to friends and family members. The ethic of justice is not all there is to morality, but it is the appropriate ethic for organizing our social and political institutions. Those holding this personal view of the ethic of care are critical of care theorists' attempts to expand the ethic of care beyond the private sphere. They argue that any attempt to expand care's scope of influence, or to make the ethic of care the whole of morality, will result in muddled thinking at best and outright corruption at worst.

A second group of critics considers the ethic of care parochial rather than personal because they consider it disappointingly limited. These critics interpret the ethic of care as an *alternative* to an ethic of justice *and*, at least as it has been developed so far, as limited to personal relations. In other words, they understand the ethic of care as limiting our moral obligations to those close to us. As a result, they criticize the ethic of care as an inappropriately narrow moral orientation. For instance, Joan Tronto writes, "It is easy to imagine that there will be some people or concerns about which we do not care. However, we might ask if our lack of care frees us from moral responsibility" (Tronto 1987, 659). At least as it has been thus far developed, the ethic of care cannot account for our moral obligations to those outside the narrow scope of our personal relationships. It fails as a moral theory because it is parochial. An adequate ethic of care would have a broader scope. But in contrast to those who regard care as a personal ethic, those who regard it as parochial do not always appeal to justice to solve this problem; rather they call for further development of the ethic of care so that it can overcome the parochialism it has displayed so far.

In this chapter I will criticize the view of the ethic of care as personal. I will do so by meeting the challenge presented by those criticizing the ethic of care as parochial. My view is that the division of care and justice ethics along public/private lines is in fact wrong: The ethic of care should not be relegated to personal relations, and the ethic of justice should not be relegated to public relations and banned from private relations. Because I believe that the argument for justice in private relations has been made effectively by others,[2] I will concentrate on the question of whether and how an ethic of care might play a role in the public sphere.

In the first section, I will show that the public/private dichotomy presupposed by the conventional boundaries of care and justice breaks down. In doing so, I will follow feminist theorists who have shown that the public and private spheres are not as separate or as different from one another as is usually thought, and thus that the public/private boundary cannot neatly divide the realms of the two ethics. However, while most feminists have focused on the ways in which the private sphere shares features usually understood as political, and thus calls for an ethic of justice, I will focus on the ways in which the public sphere shares features usually understood as private, and thus calls for an ethic of care. Thus I will argue that the ethic of care has moral implications beyond the sphere of personal relations.

In the second section, I will return to the question of whether it is possible to expand the boundaries of the ethic of care by critically examining the three standard distinctions between the two ethics. While I will accept definitions of the ethic of care and the ethic of justice based on these distinctions, I will argue that the distinctions are frequently exaggerated or misunderstood in ways that are used illegitimately to support the conventional boundaries of justice and care. I will challenge the conventional boundaries of the ethic of care by showing that the distinctive features of the ethic of care do not necessarily result in its conventional boundaries. The private ethic of care can be transformed so that it retains its distinctive features in the public sphere.

Challenging the Public/Private Dichotomy

In Chapter 1 I used the Heinz dilemma to illustrate the distinctions generally drawn between the ethic of care and the ethic of justice, distinctions used to justify the conventional boundaries of justice and care. If one ethic is properly private and the other is properly public, we ought to be able to determine which of these ethics is the correct approach in this context by determining whether the Heinz dilemma is *really* a public or a private situation. Unfortunately, this determination is itself at issue. According to Lawrence Kohlberg, the Heinz dilemma is fundamentally a public situation: Heinz's obligation to save his wife should be understood not as a personal obligation but as a universal obligation. That is, there is a universal right to life which supersedes the right to property, so Heinz's personal relationship to his wife is not morally relevant. Kohlberg writes, "It would be right to steal for a stranger because the right to life should be accorded universally to all men whose lives can be saved regardless of personal ties" (cited in Nunner-Winkler 1993, 149). While Kohlberg's emphasis on justice considerations leads him to abstract from Heinz's relationship to his wife, Gilligan's respondents' emphasis on care leads them to personalize the relationship between the Heinzes and the druggist. They point out that the dilemma arose in the first place because of the druggist's immoral failure to respond to Mrs. Heinz's need. They also suggest that Heinz personally appeal to the druggist to make his wife's condition clear to him. That is, they understand the moral problem as arising from the breakdown of personal relationships, and seek to resolve it by maintaining and building personal relationships. So the Heinz dilemma can be interpreted as either public or private, depending upon one's moral orientation.

However, neither the care nor the justice interpretations of the Heinz dilemma is able to restrict the dilemma to a single sphere. First, as Gertrud Nunner-Winkler points out, Kohlberg's argument that the right to life supersedes the right to property, regardless of personal ties, leads to a conclusion Kohlberg presumably does not accept, that we should steal to help strangers in need:

> Thus we all are not only required to give away all the money we own but also justified—in fact, maybe even obliged—to rob all banks as well as all members of our society who own more than they need to feed themselves, so as to be able to save the starving children in the third world, whose sad fate is well known to all of us. (Nunner-Winkler 1993, 149)

In order to justify Heinz's stealing for his dying wife but not for a dying stranger, or even to grant that Heinz has a *greater* obligation to save his wife's life than those of strangers, as Kohlberg presumably does, we need to recognize the moral relevance of Heinz's personal relationship to his wife. This means that the Heinz dilemma is not solely a public situation. Gilligan's respondents face a similar difficulty. When asked how Heinz's obligations would change if the dying person were not his wife but a stranger, Amy responds that "if the stranger didn't have anybody near or anybody she knew Heinz should try to save her life" (Gilligan 1982, 28). When Claire is asked whether Heinz's feelings for his wife affect his obligations, she responds that it is irrelevant whether Heinz loves his wife because she "is another human being who needs help" (Gilligan 1982, 54). Both Amy and Claire seem to base Heinz's obligation less on his personal relationship to his wife than on a general responsibility to help anyone in need. This suggests that the Heinz dilemma is not solely a personal situation.

This difficulty in categorizing the Heinz dilemma as either a public or a private situation signifies more general difficulties in drawing sharp lines between the public and the private spheres. In this section I will show how the public/private dichotomy breaks down and indicate how this undermines the conventional boundaries of justice and care.

The conventional boundaries of care and justice presuppose a public/private dichotomy, such that the public and private spheres are separate and distinct realms of activity. According to this dichotomy, the public realm tends to be characterized by self-interest, competition, and autonomy, while the private sphere tends to be characterized by altruism, interconnectedness, and dependence. As a result of their differences, each of these spheres is thought to give rise in liberal democracy to a distinctive kind of moral concern: in the public sphere, morality typically concerns the abuse of power, and in the private sphere, morality typically concerns promoting individuals' well-being. The ethic of justice, especially its negative duties of noninterference, is well-suited to handle the moral problems of the public sphere, while the ethic of care, with its active attention to individuals' needs, is well-suited to handle the moral problems of the private sphere. However, if these characterizations of the public and private spheres are mistaken, then the conventional boundaries of care and justice lose much of their rationale.

Feminists have challenged the public/private dichotomy in two ways. First, they have challenged its privileging of public relations over private relations. Public relations between relative strangers are generally considered paradigmatic moral relations, while personal relations between family and friends are considered of lesser moral importance. For instance, despite his concessions to Gilligan, Kohlberg continued to defend his view that justice, and its context of the public sphere, is central to morality. According to Kohlberg, the ethic of care may be adequate in the realm of personal relations, but in order to reach the highest level of morality, one must take part in the "secondary institutions" of society. Ultimately, that is, morality is about ordering a society justly, not about taking care of individuals. Against this, critics have pointed out that perhaps the activities of the private sphere are considered of lesser moral importance *because* they are coded as feminine. Marilyn Friedman writes:

> It seems that Kohlberg's primacy of justice reasoning coincides with the longstanding presumption of Western thought that the world of personal relationships, of the family and of familial ties and loyalties—the traditional world of women—is a world of lesser moral importance than the public world of government and of the marketplace—the male dominated world outside the home. (Friedman 1987b, 194)

Feminists have challenged this devaluation of the private sphere by showing that its distinctive activities, such as child-rearing, are essential for the continuation of a just society and thus should be recognized as central rather than peripheral in moral theory. As Baier puts it, "A decent morality will not depend for its stability on forces to which it gives no moral recognition" (Baier 1993, 25). But this is precisely what many moral philosophers do when they simply presuppose the ethic of care.

Feminists have also shown that the public and private spheres of activity are not as different from one another as is commonly assumed. For example, power relations, which are usually considered the distinguishing feature of the political, are present in personal relationships. Thirty percent of all female murder victims in 1986 were killed by their husbands or boyfriends (Okin 1989a, 129). Physical abuse is the most obvious example of power dynamics in personal relations. Yet the standard characterizations of personal relations mask the power dynamics within them. In fact, precisely because families are constituted as private, they provide distinctive opportunities for abuses of power. For this reason, personal relations must be held accountable to norms of justice. This need not mean that families be *merely* just, as critics have suggested (Sandel 1982), but that they should be *at least* just. Justice is a necessary but not a sufficient condition for good personal relations.[3] For my purposes, the point here is that because the private sphere is more like the public sphere than is usually assumed, the ethic of justice is more appropriate in the private sphere than is usually assumed.

I will make an analogous argument about the appropriateness of the ethic of care to the public sphere by showing a second way in which the public and private spheres of activity are not as different from one another as is usually assumed. I will do so in a way that also challenges the conventional view that the activities of the public sphere are morally more significant than activities of the private sphere, by treating personal relations, rather than public relations, as morally paradigmatic. In particular I will show that the moral concerns that make the ethic of care necessary in personal relations are also present outside the realm of personal relations.[4]

I will begin by exploring the moral basis of the ethic of care in personal relations, asking *why* we have obligations to care for our family and friends more than we do for people in general.[5] There are several ways to answer this question. One is to say that we should care for those close to use simply because they *are* close to us. However, while this may count as a psychological explanation, it is not a moral justification. A second response grounds our special responsibilities to care for others in our voluntary commitments to them. On this model, the paradigm moral obligation is that we should keep our promises, and other moral obligations are understood as analogous to promissory obligations. In general, the voluntarist model has the effect of limiting the scope of our moral obligations, as all obligations must be at least implicitly self-assumed. Many moral philosophers have attempted to interpret relations between friends and family on a voluntarist model (e.g., Veatch 1972, 542–43). This interpretation lends support to the conventional boundaries of care. If we can be understood as consenting to our obligations to care for friends and family, but not to people in general, the conventional boundaries of care seem to follow.

I will argue against the voluntarist model, following Robert Goodin's argument in *Protecting the Vulnerable*, that our obligations to care for family and friends are based on the fact that our family and friends are particularly *vulnerable* to our actions and choices. That is, we have special obligations to our family and friends because we can affect their interests to a great extent. But many people beyond our family and friends are *also* particularly vulnerable to our actions and choices, and thus the ethic of care has implications beyond our sphere of personal relations. Those closer to us will *tend* to be more vulnerable to our actions and choices than those distant from us, and thus we are not obliged to weigh everyone's interests exactly equally. Yet insofar as those distant from us *are* particularly vulnerable to our actions and choices, we have special obligations to care for them. And to that extent, the conventional boundaries of the ethic of care break down.

Many of our personal caring relations would be hard to fit into a voluntarist model; for instance, we do not choose our parents or our siblings, and yet most would agree that we have obligations to care for them. I will focus on personal relations which seem most likely to fit into a voluntarist model: those between spouses and between friends. We choose our spouses and our friends, and according to the voluntarist model, doing so creates our special obligations to them. In the case of spouses, the voluntary commitment is made explicit by the marriage contract. However, there are several problems with the voluntarist account of the obligations of marriage and friendship. First, the commitments associated with these relationships are not altogether voluntary. Most of the time the marriage contract is not a real contract in that people who enter marriage contracts do not negotiate their contents, and for the most part are even unaware of their contents. Likewise, the degree of choice involved in friendship is diminished by the fact that friendship requires certain feelings, and we cannot choose our feelings in any direct sense. So neither set of obligations is as chosen as it might seem.

Of course advocates of the voluntarist model would argue that marriage and friendship *ought* to be based on voluntary consent, and that care obligations are generated only to the extent that they are. This consent need not be explicit: Spouses and friends can voluntarily assume certain roles and thereby assume the responsibilities associated with those roles. However, this can at best explain *why* we have special obligations to our spouses and friends; it cannot give a complete account of them. It cannot, for instance, explain *what* our obligations to our spouses and friends are, while the vulnerability model can do so. For example, traditionally, marriage contracts have required that husbands support their wives economically. According to the vulnerability model, this is explained by the fact that traditionally, wives have been completely dependent upon their husbands for material support. The connection between dependence and obligations is reinforced by the fact that women's increasing economic independence has corresponded with changes in the marriage contract, such that women now may have the obligation to support their husbands economically.

It might be argued that individuals are vulnerable to the actions and choices of any number of people, not simply to those of their spouse or friends, and thus that the vulnerability model cannot explain our special obligations to them. To show why spouses and friends are responsible to each other *in particular*, we have to recognize their emotional vulnerabilities to one another. Even when spouses are economically independent of one another they are typically emotionally dependent upon one another, and this dependence gives rise to special responsibilities. Robert Goodin writes:

> The reason marriage partners owe each other what they do is not that they have made each other certain promises in the wedding ceremony. It is instead that they have placed themselves, emotionally and sometimes physically and economically as well in one another's power. (Goodin 1985, 79)

Likewise, part of what makes people friends is their emotional vulnerability to one another, and these vulnerabilities explain their responsibilities better than their explicit or implicit commitments to one another do. From this perspective, voluntary commitments to relationships are important because they tend to *create* vulnerabilities, but it is the vulnerabilities rather than the commitments themselves that ground care obligations. Thus the vulnerability model does not reject the voluntarist model, but subsumes it by providing a more complete account.

The vulnerability model of our care obligations undermines the conventional boundaries of care because those we know personally are not the only people particularly vulnerable to our actions and choices. For example, future generations are vulnerable to our generation, and poor and needy people, both in our country and worldwide, are vulnerable to those of us who have the means to help them. I will consider the vulnerability model's implications for the ethic of care by examining the case of starving people in foreign countries. In arguing that we have a moral obligation to send aid to them, Peter Singer compared foreign victims of famine to a drowning child (Singer 1972). He argued that just as a person on a beach has a responsibility to save a drowning child, we have the responsibility to help famine victims. In both cases, we have special responsibilities to those who are particularly vulnerable to our actions and choices: Their lives depend upon whether we choose to come to their aid.

One objection to this line of argument is that the appropriate analogy to the famine situation is a child drowning off a *crowded* beach. On this beach there are *many* individuals who could save the child, and thus the child is not *particularly* vulnerable to any one person, diminishing the responsibility of any one individual. Or, the drowning child is *particularly* vulnerable to the one person who is in the best position to help (because he or she is closest, or the best swimmer), thus diminishing everyone else's responsibility. However, as Goodin shows, the responsibility of individuals in a position to help is diminished only if and when someone else helps the needy person. While each of the bystanders would "be off the hook if any one of them acted, it is equally certain that they all remain firmly on the hook so long as none act" (Goodin, 1985, 162). "The limit of this responsibility is, quite simply, the limit of the vulnerable agent's needs and of the responsible agent's capacity to act efficaciously" (Goodin 1985, 135). Likewise, while many individuals may help the famine victims, each individual remains responsible as long as there remain victims.

This leads to a second objection to this attempt to ground moral obligations to starving foreigners on the vulnerability model: Any aid an individual might offer famine victims would make no real difference in the overall levels of world poverty. The only way to make such a difference would be to address larger social and economic issues, and this is possible only through organized collective efforts. All of this is true, but once again, the fact that there is a collective responsibility to aid famine victims does not diminish the responsibility of individuals. Rather, it means that individuals ought to exercise their responsibilities by participating in collective efforts, or if there are none, by helping to organize collective efforts (Goodin 1985, 163–4). Outside the realm of personal relations, people tend to be vulnerable to collectivities rather than to individuals. But collectivities are made up of individuals, and collective responsibilities must be understood in terms of the responsibilities of individuals.

To summarize, this argument for expanding the boundaries of the ethic of care has two parts. First, our care obligations within the private sphere are based on our friends' and family members' vulnerabilities to us. Second, people beyond our private sphere are *also* vulnerable to our actions and choices, and thus we also have care obligations to them. This argument challenges one aspect of the public/private dichotomy—the view that each sphere, because of its distinctive nature, calls for its own ethic. Others have challenged this view in one way by showing that the moral concerns that call for an ethic of justice are present in private as well as in public. I have challenged it in another way by showing that the moral concerns that call for an ethic of care are present in public as well as in private. The ethic of care has moral implications beyond the sphere of personal relations. However, I have not yet addressed the arguments made against expanding the boundaries of care. I will turn to these in the next section.

Challenging the Conventional Boundaries of Care

Gilligan's respondents who used an ethic of care often extended it to the public sphere. As Susan Moller Okin observes:

> Many of those who speak in this voice use it to express as fully universalizable a morality of social concern as respondents who express themselves very differently, using the language of justice and rights. (Okin 1990, 159)

However, those defending the conventional boundaries of justice and care would be unimpressed by this observation. They would suggest that those who apply the ethic of care universally are confused about the appropriate boundaries of care: Although they may use the language of care, they really express the ethic of justice. In Chapter 1 I showed that according to the ideal type of care, the distinguishing features of the ethic of care are possible, moral and/or helpful only within the context of personal relations. Against this standard account, I now want to show that those who apply the ethic of care in public contexts can instead be understood as making important challenges to the appropriateness of the conventional boundaries of care. In this section I will argue that the three distinguishing features of the ethic of care need not limit it to personal contexts. I will also show that these distinctions between the ethic of care and the ethic of justice are often exaggerated or mistaken in ways that lend illegitimate support to the conventional public/private boundaries. The relegation of the ethic of care to personal contexts is not an inevitable result of its features, but rather a consequence of a common misinterpretation and devaluation of its features.

The Abstract/Concrete Distinction

As I showed in Chapter 1, the distinction between the abstractness of the ethic of justice and the concreteness of the ethic of care seems at first to support conventional public/private boundaries because attention to individuating details is thought to be possible and/or desirable only in the context of personal relations. This conclusion only seems to follow, however, because of common misunderstandings of the distinction between the abstractness of justice and the concreteness of care.

Contrary to the prevailing view, the difference between the abstractness of the ethic of justice and the concreteness of the ethic of care is a difference in emphasis, not in kind. The ethic of care focuses on the particularities of a situation because it recognizes the dangers of applying general rules without regard for individuals and their specific needs. Advocates of the ethic of care frequently cite examples of highly principled men who sacrifice individuals for the sake of their principles; Abraham's willingness to sacrifice Isaac is often interpreted in this way. For its part, the ethic of justice focuses on the general principles which underlie our apparently dissimilar moral judgments because it recognizes the dangers of being so immersed in context that one loses sight of one's principles and becomes inconsistent and/or relativistic. However, although the two ethics focus on different dangers, they are not opposites. Properly understood, the ethic of justice requires not just abstract principles but contextual details as well. Likewise, the ethic of care requires not only contextual details but general principles as well. Moreover, the contextuality of the ethic of care need not result in moral relativism.

In fact, regardless of one's moral orientation, neither general principles nor contextual detail should be seen as ultimately settling moral questions. Most commonly, of course, moral philosophers assume that general principles settle moral conflicts. But different general principles conflict with one another in particular cases, and such conflicts can only be settled through attention to context. That is, general principles and contextual detail are dependent upon one another. Attention to detail helps us formulate, select, and apply general principles, which in turn put the details in moral perspective and thus help us select which details are relevant for our consideration. (Jaggar 1994, 9) Contrary to the ideal types of justice and care, neither an abstract nor a concrete approach can function alone.

First, in order to discern which principles of justice apply in a particular situation, one must pay attention to its contextual details. Kohlberg would certainly agree that some amount of contextual detail is necessary to identify the applicable principle of justice at stake in a situation. He believes that he has provided enough detail in the Heinz dilemma to point to the principle that the right to life overrides the right to property. However, as Marilyn Friedman points out, depending upon how the Heinz dilemma is further fleshed out, this may or may not be the appropriate principle. Suppose that Heinz's wife has become "disfigured in a manner that she has never been able to accept, weakened, and in pain from the cancer that continues to poison her body, bedridden and dependent on others for her daily functioning" such that "she has lost hope and grown despondent at a fate which, to her, is worse than death" (Friedman 1987b, 201). In this case, the relevant principle is not the priority of life over property, but rather the right to choose to end one's own life. This attention to details about Mrs. Heinz is not just the nonmoral preliminary to the distinctively moral process of applying an abstract principle, but is itself a moral process. A truly just person, not just a caring person, is one whose judgments arise out of close attention to contextual details. Deciding which principles are relevant and what priority to give them requires full attention to context.

Similar points can be made about the process of *applying* moral principles. One's moral responsibilities are not exhausted once one has discerned that the appropriate principle in the Heinz dilemma is that life takes priority over property. As Kohlberg constructs the dilemma, the only way to apply this principle is to break into the drugstore and steal the drug. But an attention to context might reveal that this is not the most just application of this principle. For instance, some of the women Gilligan interviewed were concerned that stealing the drug might cause more harm than good, since Heinz might be jailed, and thus his wife might be abandoned when she needs his companionship most. Because of such considerations, these women suggested other possible applications of the same principle, such as, for instance, that Heinz might take out a bank loan so he can buy the drug for his wife. In other words, all applications of a moral principle are not equally just, and the most just application is one based on a sensitivity to context.

Still other contextual details would suggest broader applications of the principle giving life priority over property. Attention to the social situation in Heinz's society would reveal that it is not just Mrs. Heinz who suffers from inadequate medical care; that there is not just an individual injustice here, but a social injustice. Thus the principle that life takes priority over property requires much more than that Heinz break the law, if need be, to preserve his wife's life. It requires that we criticize not only the greedy druggist, but the social system that allows his greed to prevent Mrs. Heinz from receiving needed health care. That is, in order to address the *real* justice problem in the Heinz dilemma, we must ask broad questions about various alternative systems for delivering health care. (Friedman 1987b, 202–204) Deciding which of these is the most just in turn requires attention to a vast array of social, economic, and political details.

In short, an attention to contextual details is important not only for an ethic of care but for an ethic of justice as well. Kai Nielsen summarizes this argument when he writes:

> Without some concrete understanding of specific people, young and old, sick and well, marginalized or mainstream, religious or secular, powerful or powerless, in their distinctive and importantly variable and changing circumstances, we can give very little *substance* to our belief that the life of everyone matters and matters equally. (Nielsen 1987, 395)

This concrete understanding is necessary to discern not only which principles of justice apply in a given case but how best to apply them. The point is that attention to contextual detail is not simply a mechanical and morally unimportant process but a crucial part of being a just person.

However, principles are also important to morality, and some theories of care tend to dismiss them too hastily. Nel Noddings holds that the ethic of care involves no principles at all. As Tong summarizes Noddings's position, "We must reject rules and principles as major guides to ethical behavior and with them the accompanying notion of universalizability" (Tong 1993, 110). In particular, Noddings maintains that the more concrete and detailed our knowledge of a situation, the less we need general principles, since a judgment *emerges* from a more and more detailed look at the situation. In short, if you have enough information, principles become unnecessary. However, Noddings interprets principles too narrowly. She understands abstract thinking to preclude contextual thinking. But it need not. Some form of abstraction is necessary to *all* thinking. As Linda Nicholson puts it, *abstraction*, which is basic to all human language competence, should be distinguished from *abstract formalism*, which is typified by the separation of form from content, and is a "specifically western mode of thinking allied to a separation of domestic and nondomestic spheres of activity" (Nicholson 1993, 93).

Noddings also makes the common mistake of equating principles with principles of justice. This is easy to do, since the principles of care are generally unexpressed and unrecognized as principles. Grimshaw illustrates this point with a story of a married couple who both disapprove of their daughter's decision to live with her boyfriend without getting married; both parents accept the same moral principle. However, while the father acts on this principle by cutting off his relationship with his daughter, the mother maintains her relationship with her daughter despite her opposition to her daughter's choice. Although it is possible to interpret the man as principled and the woman as non-principled, this ignores the fact that the woman's actions may result from a second principle to which she gives priority, a principle requiring her to maintain her relationship with her daughter. Grimshaw writes:

> I suspect that it is sometimes the case, not that women do not act on principles, but that the principles on which they act are not recognized as valid or important ones. Thus, to act so as to maintain relationships, despite a belief that a certain behavior is wrong, may be seen as a weakness, as a failure of principle. It may, however, more adequately be represented as a difference of priorities. (Grimshaw 1986, 210)

When we recognize that principles need not entail abstract formalism or a justice orientation, it becomes clear that principles are important even to an ethic of care.

The attention to contextual detail characteristic of the ethic of care is often interpreted as relativism, or as the view that there is no correct way of resolving moral dilemmas. Even Carol Gilligan seems to accept this view at times, as when she writes that those who use the ethic of care have "difficulty in arriving at definitive answers to moral judgments" (Gilligan 1982, 101). This interpretation of the ethic of care as relativistic lends support to the conventional boundaries of care because it is generally thought that in the private sphere, and only in the private sphere, relativism is acceptable: We do not need to reach universal agreement about our individual life choices in the way we must about the structure of society. But one need not be a moral relativist to be unwilling to take a stand on the Heinz dilemma as it is presented. As I have argued, justice as well as care requires close attention to the details of a situation, more attention than the Heinz dilemma provides. Regardless of one's moral orientation, one needs contextual detail to know which principles to apply as well as how to apply those principles. The reluctance to make a moral judgment is healthy when one knows minimal details of a situation. As Friedman puts it:

> Sensitivity to contextual detail need not carry with it the relativistic view that there are no moral rights or wrongs, nor the slightly weaker view that there is no way to decide what is right or wrong. It need only be associated with uncertainties about

which principles to apply in a particular case, or a concern that one does not yet know enough to apply one's principles, or a worry that one's principles are too narrow to deal with the novelties at hand. (Friedman 1987b, 203)

The ethic of care's attention to detail is not a weakness resulting in relativism, but a strength lacking in simplistic versions of the ethic of justice.

Let me turn now to the question of whether the contextuality of the ethic of care limits it to the private sphere. I have already shown that an ethic of justice should also be contextual, and that the ethic of care is not only contextual but principled as well. But the ethic of care still places special emphasis on taking the standpoint of the concrete other, in which one focuses on the particular features of individuals in making moral decisions. The question, then, is whether it is possible to take the standpoint of the concrete other in the context of public decisionmaking. It is clear that in practice it would be impossible to focus on the particular features of each and every individual affected by public policy decisions in the way we focus on the particular features of intimates in making personal caring decisions. This might lead us to conclude that the ethic of care's concreteness has no application in the public sphere.

However, while public policy decisions do not allow for attention to particular features of *individuals*, they do allow for attention to distinguishing features of *groups*. Nancy Fraser suggests that we recognize the standpoint of the "collective concrete other" in which we "abstract both from unique individuality *and* from universal humanity to focalize the intermediate zone of group identity" (Fraser 1986, 427–8). For instance, in the Heinz dilemma, Heinz's wife could be seen as belonging to a group of people whose medical treatment is beyond their financial means. Her pre-existing membership in other groups would also be relevant. For example, if she were a Christian Scientist, this would have important implications for decisions about her medical care. The fact that we do not know the individual particularities of the members of such a group would not prevent us from focusing on the group's special needs in making public policy. In this form, the concrete standpoint of the ethic of care is possible in the public sphere. The contextual emphasis of the ethic of care need not limit it to the sphere of personal relations.

The Distinction in Priorities

The ethic of justice prioritizes equality in some form, while the ethic of care prioritizes maintaining one's relationships to others and meeting the needs of those to whom one is related. Like the first distinction between the two ethics, this distinction is often misinterpreted in ways that support the conventional boundaries. In particular, these priorities are generally understood as opposed to one another. Advocates of the ethic of care often imply that all ethics of justice are alike in focusing on a particularly narrow interpretation of equality. For example, Gilligan's interpretation of the ethic of justice focuses exclusively on its attention to negative rights, or rights of noninterference. As Susan Moller Okin writes,

"She tends therefore to conflate talk about rights with individualism and even selfishness" (Okin 1990, 157). If justice has the limited goal of noninterference, then it is clearly inappropriate for our personal relations, in which it is uncontroversial that we have positive responsibilities. And, if rights are individualistic and selfish, then there is no room for rights in the ethic of care. Similarly, if the priorities of the ethic of care are understood to preclude equal rights, the ethic seems ill-suited for public contexts. If justice and care have mutually exclusive priorities, they must have separate and distinct spheres of application.

However, justice and care priorities can overlap in endorsing positive rights. Although a libertarian ethic of justice focuses exclusively on negative rights, other ethics of justice, ranging from liberal to socialist, defend positive rights, or rights that entail correlative obligations to provide the rights holder with some benefit. And although certain versions of the ethic of care reject the concept of rights, others interpret care priorities in terms of positive rights.[6] Rita Manning writes, "there is no reason why we couldn't adopt a language of rights to further the commitments of care. Indeed the blossoming of the language of positive rights seems designed for this purpose" (Manning 1992, 154). An ethic of care which prioritizes certain positive rights has obvious applications in public contexts. Virginia Held cites some of these:

> We ought to acknowledge that our fellow citizens and fellow inhabitants of the globe have moral rights to what they need to live—to the food, shelter, and medical care that are the necessary conditions of living and growing—and that when the resources exist for honoring such rights there are few excuses for not doing so. Such rights are not rights to be left to starve unimpeded. (Held 1987b, 129)[7]

The suggestion that public policy be guided by the priorities of care need not mean that these priorities should replace equality, the priority of the ethic of justice. Instead, the priorities of care can guide us toward a specific conception of justice. Different conceptions of justice appeal to different conceptions of equality, ranging from the equal right to use one's resources as one chooses to the equal right to have one's basic needs met. Bringing the priorities of care to the public sphere leads us to favor an idea of justice based on positive rights rather than negative rights alone. In other words, in this context the important distinction is not between justice and care, but between the kind of rights that public policy promotes.

This emphasis on positive rights gives rise, however, to another argument against using an ethic of care in public contexts, namely that the ethic of care is ill-equipped to deal with the moral conflicts characteristic of the public sphere. In order to resolve conflicting claims over the division of scarce resources, critics argue, we do not need moral principles which advise us to meet everyone's needs, but ones which advise us of how to make fair decisions when it is impossible to meet everyone's needs. For instance, since it is impossible for Heinz to care for both his wife and the druggist, critics argue that Heinz must dispense with an ethic of care and make use of an ethic of justice which ranks his wife's right to life against the druggist's right to property.

There are several problems with this argument. One is its assumption that rights conflicts are exclusive to the public sphere. Rights conflicts also arise in the context of personal relationships, and thus an ethic of justice should not be restricted to public contexts. Also, while the ethic of justice focuses more directly than the ethic of care on conflict resolution, the ethic of justice cannot always settle conflict cases. Often principles of justice conflict, and there is no accepted metaprinciple to help in the choice between them. In addition, care priorities can also help us resolve conflict in nonviolent ways by promoting attention to and discussion of needs. As Kathy Ferguson writes:

> The accommodative strategies of conflict resolution that women typically use would be encouraged and legitimized, calling on the cooperative and respectful processes of talking and listening that express care and maintain connection. (Ferguson 1984, 198)

Thus it is a mistake to think that the ethic of justice can always or exclusively settle conflicts.

It is also a mistake to limit morality to conflict resolution. The ethic of care focuses on *preventing* conflicts. Preventing conflicts seems at least as important as resolving conflicts that have already arisen, and is not restricted to one sphere of activity. Gilligan shows how the ethic of care can prevent conflict when she examines the 1917 short story, "A Jury of Her Peers," by Susan Glaspell (Gilligan 1987, 29–31). In this story, a man has been killed, and his wife, Minnie Foster, is accused of the murder. The sheriff and the prosecutor, both men, search the house for evidence necessary to convict the suspect. The two women who accompany them, a neighbor woman and the sheriff's wife, collect the things Minnie Foster will need in jail, in the process taking note of the similarities between this home and their own, and uncovering a strangled canary. Concluding that Minnie Foster has killed her husband because he killed the bird she loved, the women see the murder as the ultimate result of Minnie Foster's isolation. Rather than judging her for the crime, they judge themselves for their failure to reach out to her before the crime. One says, "I *wish* I'd come over here once in a while. That was a crime! Who's going to punish that?" (Gilligan 1987, 29–30) The ethic of justice offers us tools for judging Minnie Foster's crime: It is wrong to kill a man because he killed a bird. But in order to prevent this crime, we need an ethic of care and its recognition of the importance of human connection in helping *avoid* injustice.

We can make the same points about the Heinz dilemma. Critics say that the ethic of care is unhelpful here: Heinz cannot care for both his wife and the druggist, so he needs to rank his wife's right to life against the druggist's right to property. But, as some of Gilligan's respondents insisted, by the time we reach the conflict between Mrs. Heinz's life and the druggist's property, morality has already in some sense broken down and violence is inevitable. The important moral issues arose prior to this dilemma: The druggist should have responded to the woman's need, and, failing that, Heinz should have reached out to others who could help. These moral issues need not concern only the three individuals identified in the dilemma. Gilligan's Amy recognized the importance of caring priorities in preventing injustice when she said, "The world should just share things more and then people wouldn't have to steal" (Gilligan 1982, 29). While this assertion is simplistic, it is undeniable that behind most outbreaks of violence and injustice is a history of abandonment and lack of care.

Just as in my earlier discussion of rights, I do not mean that these care priorities should *replace* justice priorities in resolving conflicts, but that care and justice priorities are not necessarily in conflict. Care priorities need not undermine justice priorities, but can help us distinguish between better and worse versions of justice, so they need not be relegated to the private sphere. Even where care priorities are especially distinctive, they can play an important role in the public sphere.

The Distinction Between Concepts of the Self

Finally, I will consider the implications of the different conceptions of the self implicit in ethic of justice and the ethic of care for the ethics' relative boundaries. Again, the ethic of justice begins with an assumption of human separateness, while the ethic of care begins with an assumption of human connectedness. The social conception of the self is used to restrict the ethic of care to personal relationships in one of two ways. First, it is thought to be psychologically impossible to experience oneself as connected to all human beings, implying that we cannot be expected to care for everyone. Second, critics argue that any public version of the ethic of care would incorporate this inevitable bias toward those in some sense close to us, and thus it would be morally wrong to rely on a social conception of the self in political decisionmaking. A public morality, critics argue, must be impartial, and an ethic of care is inevitably partial.

The distinction between impartial and partial moral theories has been interpreted in a way that is misleading, in particular as suggesting that impartial moral theories do not allow for any partiality toward family and friends. According to this extreme interpretation, Heinz would have no more obligation to his dying wife than he does to dying strangers. As I noted earlier, sometimes Kohlberg seems to endorse such a view. In reaction to this interpretation, a number of moral philosophers have recently offered defenses of partiality toward family and friends.[8] They have argued that this kind of partiality, or "taking care of one's own," is not only morally permissible, but morally required. However, as Marilyn Friedman points out, there are very few defenders of the extreme interpretation of impartiality that these partialists oppose. Peter Singer (1979) does argue that we ought to give equal consideration to the interests of all individuals (human and otherwise), but as Marilyn Friedman argues (1991), almost no one takes this extreme position. Most "impartialists" believe that in many contexts it is legitimate for us to give more weight to the interests of our friends and family members than to those of strangers. The debate is over *how* this partiality is justified, not *whether* it is justified. The ethic of care and the ethic of justice do not differ with regard to whether partiality is ever justified. Yet while the partiality toward family and friends allowed by various ethics of justice is not thought to rule out concern for the needs of strangers, the partiality allowed by the ethic of care is thought to do so.

Friedman gives one reason to think that the ethic of care does not rule out global moral concern when she distinguishes between the feminist partialism of the ethic of care and other nonfeminist partialisms. Nonfeminist partialists actually *oppose* the notion of global moral concern; they "argue that special obligations to those who are close to us, to those who are 'our own' should virtually eclipse those distant obligations in our attention" (Friedman 1991, 174). In contrast, feminist partialists "have endorsed partiality not so much for its own sake but rather as part of a larger project" of promoting esteem for women's traditional caring activities (Friedman 1991, 164). Thus when feminists challenge moral impartiality, they are challenging the reasoning *methods* of impartialist theories which regard a sense of social connection as an impediment to morality; they are not challenging the global moral *scope* of impartialist theories. Indeed, compared to nonfeminist partialists,

> Feminist partialists devote much more theoretical attention to developing concern for those who are not "one's own." . . . Cross-cultural connections, theoretical and practical, are highly revered feminist achievements. Thus for feminists, "global moral concern" does not mean the practice of exactly equal consideration of the interests of all individuals; but it does mean substantially more concern for distant or different peoples than is common in our culture and our time. (Friedman 1991, 175)

Friedman shows that feminists defending the ethic of care are not motivated by the desire to rule out global concern, and in fact are quite concerned about promoting global concern.

However, good intentions aside, this leaves the question of whether the ethic of care *is conceptually able* to allow for global moral concern, or whether, as its critics argue, it inevitably fails to do so because of its reliance on a social conception of the self. They argue that since we experience ourselves as unconnected to most people in the world, if we are to acknowledge any moral obligation to those distant from us, we must appeal to an ethic of justice. In short, justice is necessary because of the limitations of the ethic of care.

I will address two parts of this argument separately, beginning with its claim that we cannot care for distant people whom we do not and never will know. Although it is certainly true that one cannot care for strangers in the sense that one cares for intimates, one can nonetheless experience oneself as connected with, and take an active interest in, those one will never know personally. In fact, the two kinds of caring are related, as we learn to care for distant others by first developing close relationships to nearby others, and then recognizing the similarities between close and distant others. As Virginia Held puts it, one learns what it is like for children close to home to starve, and then one recognizes that distant children are like those close to home (Held 1987a, 118). A woman in Gilligan's study extends her sense of social connection to *everyone* when she says that Heinz's obligations to his wife are not based on his feelings for her, because his wife "is another human being who needs help." She goes on to explain that, "Although a person may not like someone else, you have to love someone else, because you are inseparable from them. In a way it's like loving your right hand; it is part of you. That other person is part of that giant collection of everybody" (Gilligan 1982, 57). While the universality of this statement may make it seem like an expression of justice, not care, it is clear that this woman has a social rather than an individualistic conception of the self. Her concern for others grows out of her sense that she is inseparable from them.

Next I will turn to the argument that the ethic of care's conception of the self limits it such that justice is morally necessary in public contexts. A public ethic of care certainly *could* take the form of nepotism or racism, and the ethic of justice is important because it unequivocally condemns such bad partialisms. But it is a mistake to assume that these are the only forms a public ethic of care might take. In fact, the limitations of the ethic of justice make the ethic of care necessary. Unless we feel a sense of connection to those who have justice claims on us, those justice claims will not matter to us. Although this may be a psychological rather than a strictly moral point, it makes an important difference for whether we carry out our justice obligations. Noddings recognizes this when she writes that "Even if we all agreed that it is unjust for some people to starve, it would still require people who care to put things right" (Noddings 1990b, 121). Virginia Held makes a similar point when she writes, "What often appears to happen is the following: When people with social privileges come to understand what the practical implications are of the conceptions of justice they think they endorse, they often give up these conceptions of justice" (Held 1985, 33). I think this happens because people's conceptions of justice are empty without a sense of social connection. My claim is that, far from undermining our relations of justice to people distant from us, care helps us recognize our justice obligations to those distant from us. This is not to say that we do not have moral obligations to those for whom we do not care; we do. But, if we want to take these obligations seriously, we should try to extend our sense of social connection by eliminating the barriers, such as ignorance, that make us feel disconnected from those physically and culturally distant from us.

Assuming that we can develop this expanded sense of social connection and that it does generate in us an awareness of obligations to those in need, both nearby and distant, another objection may arise: We cannot possibly care for everyone who needs it. Once we extend the boundaries of care beyond our sphere of personal relations and beyond our voluntary associations, we become overburdened by obligations. The ethic of care requires too much of us.

On the one hand, it is hard to take this objection too seriously when it comes from a privileged minority who think they, in contrast to the underprivileged majority from whom they benefit, have a right to choose their burdens. As Rita Manning writes, "In the face of glaring maldistribution of the world's resources and the resultant suffering of the world's poor, the complaint of the affluent that they are overburdened by obligations to care sounds suspiciously like whining" (Manning 1992, 147). On the other hand, given the inequitable distribution of care work in our society, this objection is important from a feminist perspective. As I showed in Chapter 2, a feminist ethic of care must allow for the caregiver's autonomy. This means that we must care for ourselves as well as others, by, for instance, taking time to pursue our own projects. While we pursue our own projects, we must continue to recognize the moral minimums set by the ethic of justice. But beyond placing personal limits on our caregiving, we need what Manning calls a politics of care, which restructures society so that caregiving is supported rather than exploited.

In this section I have challenged the conventional boundaries of the ethic of care by showing that none of the ethic's three distinguishing features entail the necessity of limiting it to the sphere of personal relations. First, I have argued that a public ethic of care can take a concrete perspective by focusing on the distinguishing features of groups. For instance, the Heinz dilemma should lead us to address the social problem of inadequate health care by focusing on the group of people who, like Heinz's wife, are deprived of health care because they cannot afford it. Second, I have shown that care priorities can be understood in terms of positive rights, so that in arguing that people have a *right* to health care, we are appealing to the priorities of the ethic of care (as well as to the priorities of many ethics of justice). Third, I have argued that it is not only possible that we extend our sense of social connection to those distant from us, but that doing so is important because it helps us recognize our moral obligations toward them. Thus I think there are good reasons to think that Gilligan's respondents who applied the ethic of care in non-personal contexts were not confused, but were making the important suggestion that we expand the boundaries of the ethic of care.

Conclusion

Given traditional sex roles, the conventional boundaries of care and justice mean that the traditional world of men should be governed by justice, while the traditional world of women should be governed by care. It is uncontroversial, among feminists at any rate, that women should have equal opportunities to men in public institutions such as the workplace. What is controversial, even among feminists, is whether the limitation of the ethic of care to personal relations is a result of the same sexism that has relegated women to the private sphere. Should the ethic of care be permitted entrance into the public sphere? Advocates of the traditional boundaries of justice and care would defend themselves against charges of sexism. They would point out that there is nothing intrinsically female about the private sphere or about the ethic of care, and that any attempt to restrict women to either is morally wrong. Men and women should have equal access to the public sphere, and both men and women should use the ethic of justice in public contexts. The restriction of the ethic of care to personal relations is not sexist, they argue, but a necessary result of the features of the ethic of care. The ethic of care is appropriate only in the context of personal relations.

In this chapter, I have challenged the conventional boundaries of care by showing that taking the ethic of care seriously requires expanding it beyond the private sphere. I have shown that it is not only *possible* to make use of the ethic of care in public contexts, but that the moral basis of the ethic of care *requires* that we do so. This argument lends implicit support to those feminists who hold that the ethic of care is given such a limited scope not because it is a necessarily personal ethic but because it is coded as feminine, and thus as subordinate. As Carol Gilligan has recently written, "When I hear care discussed as a matter of special obligations or as an ethic of interpersonal relationships, I hear the vestiges of patriarchy" (Gilligan 1995, 125). I have shown that the restriction of the ethic of care to personal contexts results from a failure to take its moral implications seriously.

So far I have discussed the possibility of expanding the boundaries of the ethic of care primarily with regard to a single hypothetical example, the Heinz Dilemma. I have done this in order to focus my discussion, but it also seems to limit the practical relevance of my argument. In the next chapter I will examine two specific public policy issues to show how the ethic of care might be applied in public contexts and to consider some of the moral issues that arise in doing so. Then, in the final chapter, I will defend an alternative to the conventional account of the relationship between the ethic of care and the ethic of justice.

Notes

1. In this public/private dichotomy, government is the paradigm of the public sphere, while the family is the paradigm of the private sphere. The realm of socioeconomic activity is sometimes considered private, and sometimes considered public. In this chapter I will group this socioeconomic realm with the public, and I will include personal relations between friends within the private.

2. E.g., Okin (1989a), Friedman (1987a), Held (1995).

3. Many different outcomes may be just in different ways, and in a family the search is often to find a form of justice compatible with care (e.g., provision according to need).

4. I will be appropriating much of the argument of Robert Goodin in *Protecting the Vulnerable* (1985), although he makes his argument solely in terms of justice, and does not discuss the ethic of care. I will provide only a general sketch of an argument that Goodin

devotes a book to developing. Although I find Goodin's argument convincing, my purpose is not to provide a complete examination or defense of this argument, but to show the implications of Goodin's project for my own. For a valuable criticism of Goodin from a care perspective, see Tronto 1993.

5. I will discuss this obligation further in the second section.

6. I believe that an ethic of care can also endorse certain negative rights, but I will not discuss that here.

7. See also Frazer and Lacey 1993, 191.

8. See Friedman's review of these (1991).

5

Public Applications
of the Ethic of Care

In Chapter 4 I argued that, contrary to the views of many moral and political philosophers, there is no conceptual reason that an ethic of care cannot be applied in public contexts. I argued that a public version of the ethic of care is possible, and, by showing the ways in which a private ethic of care *implies* a public ethic of care, I suggested that it is also desirable. I have not yet examined any particular version of a public ethic of care in depth, nor have I considered the range of possible public ethics of care. In fact, few commentators have tried to address these questions. As Onora O'Neill recently wrote:

> While phrases such as "caring society," "community care," or "commitment to care" have become clichés of contemporary public debate, its relations to justice and its import in a world of mediated social relations where need and poverty are often at a distance from those who could reduce them, have not yet been convincingly elaborated. (O'Neill 1992, 136)

In this chapter, I will begin the process of elaborating on what might be meant by a caring society, or a public ethic of care. In doing so I will return to a number of the themes of the work as a whole, illustrating and reinforcing some of the arguments I have made in previous chapters. This chapter will clarify the relationship between care and autonomy, both in theory and practice. It will also continue to consider the relationship between care and justice, and the related relationships between public and private spheres of activity and between abstract and concrete styles of thinking.

I will examine two different possible public ethics of care. In Section 1 I will examine the idea that the ethic of care supports political pacifism, and in particular the "maternal pacifism" of Sara Ruddick. In Section 2 I will examine social welfare programs in general and the public funding of long-term care for the elderly in particular. I will ask three interrelated questions about these two proposals. First, I will ask *whether* they can be understood as versions of the ethic of care. This becomes a question because public applications of the ethic of care are not generally defended in the language of care. In these cases I will consider whether arguments made in terms of maternal thinking and justice can be understood as arguments about the ethic of care. If a policy takes a contextual approach, is based on a social conception of the self, and prioritizes maintaining relationships and meeting individual needs, then I will call it a version of the ethic of care, regardless of what its advocates call it. In particular I will argue that pacifism, as it is usually defined, does not truly exemplify the ethic of care because of its excessive abstractness, but that an alternative, what Ruddick calls contextual pacifism, does. I will also argue that, at their best, social welfare programs do exemplify the defining features of the ethic of care.

In examining these proposed versions of the ethic of care, I will also distinguish between better and worse versions of the ethic of care. In previous chapters I have shown that a satisfactory ethic of care must allow for the autonomy of both care recipients and care providers. Here I will show that attention to the role of autonomy illuminates the debates surrounding both proposals I will examine. In the first case, I will show that while standard forms of pacifism are implied by the conventional level of care, they are not implied by an ethic of care which allows for a carer's autonomy. Then, in examining the public funding of long-term care for the elderly, I will consider the charge that this public application of the ethic of care undermines its corresponding private application; that welfare programs threaten the family. Against this, I will argue that such programs actually support rather than threaten "family values," at least the healthy family values of genuine rather than distorted care; that is, of autonomous rather than nonautonomous care.

The third question I will address concerns the relationship between care and justice. I will show that in these contexts, care and justice should not be understood as mutually exclusive. Rather, they should be understood as checks upon one another, such that both of the ethics are necessary for an adequate approach to morality. Thus the most important question will not be whether a proposal instantiates the ethic of care *or* the ethic of justice, but whether it instantiates a version of the ethic of care that is informed by justice concerns (or an ethic of justice informed by care concerns). I will show that pacifism is flawed to the extent that it is defined in opposition to a justice-based approach, and that ideally the two approaches influence one another. In my examination of welfare policies, I will show that the ethic of care's social conception of the self requires that welfare programs address relational concerns that are not generally addressed by individualistic approaches. For a satisfactory welfare policy we must not only determine who is entitled to how much of what; we must also pay close attention to the quality of the relationships between caregivers and care recipients.

Maternal Pacifism

Perhaps because of their role as childcare givers, women have often been thought to be more peaceful than men, and "women's morality" is often associated with pacifism. Moreover, probably the most well-known attempt to apply the ethic of care in public contexts is Sara Ruddick's argument that the practice of mothering implies political pacifism. In this section I will give an overview of Ruddick's accounts of maternal thinking and pacifism, and examine her arguments for connecting the two. I will show that there are problems with the attempt to link maternal thinking and pacifism, at least when pacifism is defined (as it usually is) as the absolute renunciation of violence. In fact, standard pacifism is morally problematic in the same way that a conventional ethic of care is. However, Ruddick's work shows that the ethic of care, as expressed in maternal thinking, supports an alternative form of pacifism that makes nonviolence a moral priority rather than an absolute rule.

Much of Ruddick's work is an exploration of the practice of mothering. Although it is mainly women who have devoted themselves to this practice, Ruddick believes that men as well as women can (and should) do so. According to Ruddick, maternal practice embodies three main priorities or ends: the preservation, the growth, and the acceptability of one's children. Each of these priorities, in turn, embodies certain maternal virtues. The priority of preserving one's child's well-being requires the virtues of scrutiny, humility, and cheerfulness. Scrutiny in particular requires careful attention to the potential threats to a child's well-being. Because a threat to one child's well-being might not be a threat to another child's well-being, such preservative love must be attuned to the particularities of each child. Fostering one's child's growth requires the virtue of realism about that child's specific strengths and weaknesses. Promoting the acceptability of one's child can give rise to the vice of unreflective acceptance of one's culture's dominant values, but Ruddick argues that doing so *authentically* requires the virtue of moral reflection on those values. With its distinctive priorities and virtues, maternal practice requires and promotes a distinctive style of thinking that Ruddick calls maternal thinking. Maternal thinking reflects the contextuality, the priorities, and the social conception of the self distinctive of the ethic of care: It requires careful attention to context, a commitment to meeting the needs of one's child, and requires a response to a reality—a child's demands—that appears to be "given" rather than chosen (Ruddick 1983a, 214).

Ruddick argues that maternal thinking has political implications. In particular, the logic of maternal thinking leads to pacifism. She defines pacifism as follows:

> A commitment to avoid battle whenever possible, to fight necessary battles nonviolently, and to take, as the aim of battle, reconciliation between opponents and restoration of connection and community. (Ruddick 1983b, 239)

She goes on to define "violence" as that which is intended to damage an opponent, and "damage" as harm, either physical or psychological, for which there is no compensatory benefit to the person damaged. Thus pacifism requires the absolute renunciation of violence, regardless of its apparent necessity or the benefits it promises others. Violence is never an acceptable means to a nonviolent end; for pacifists, means and ends are inseparable. However, the renunciation of violence does not require that one passively accept whatever violence others choose to inflict. In particular, pacifism allows for nonviolent resistance in the forms of civil disobedience, noncooperation, boycotts, strikes, etc. These nonviolent forms of resistance are intended to appeal to the conscience of one's aggressors, or, if that fails, to their reputation in the eyes of others.

Next I will consider the arguments Ruddick offers to show that maternal thinking implies pacifism. First, I should emphasize that Ruddick's arguments concern the *logic* of maternal thinking rather than the practices or commitments of actual mothers. That is, Ruddick does not deny the fact that mothers are often violent toward their children, nor that mothers are often as supportive of their nations' political violence as are nonmothers. However, she argues that according to the logic of maternal thinking, mothers should not be violent toward their children, and should not support state-sanctioned violence. Mothers who participate in or endorse violence are not acting *as* mothers.

In order to evaluate it, I will divide Ruddick's general argument into two distinct arguments. The first of these focuses on the conflicts between the *goals* of maternal practice and the *goals* of war. The second argument holds that the *concreteness* of maternal thinking conflicts with the *abstractness* of military thinking.

Ruddick's first argument focuses on the preservative love of maternal practice. Mothers strive to preserve the life and health of their children. In contrast, military strategy is willing to sacrifice the lives of these children (or young people) in order to achieve ends deemed good for the nation. Thus, military thinking threatens the very thing that maternal thinking tries to preserve. Ruddick writes:

> On the one side, we have maternal practice whose end is defined by the demand to preserve what is both treasured and at risk. On the other side we have military practice which puts at risk those same treasured lives in the name of "victory" or other abstract causes. (Ruddick 1983b, 241)

According to Ruddick, the conflicting objectives of maternal and military practices establish a connection between maternal practice and pacifism: In the interest of preserving their children's lives, mothers should oppose war, and embrace pacifism.

Certainly, preservative love would conflict with sending one's child to war. But preservative love would equally require protecting one's child, with violence if necessary, from that which threatens him or her. Most immediately, this might mean defending one's child against an attacker. But also, if social conditions are so bad that one's child's life or well-being are threatened, a mother's preservative love may lead her to encourage others to fight to change those conditions and thereby help her child (Davion 1990, 93–94). In general, a mother's commitment to the well-being of her children may lead her to use or condone violence toward those she perceives as threats to them. Ruddick recognizes that mothers are willing to use violence against those they perceive as threats to their children. Yet she attributes such violence to unjustified fears:

> Class, racial, neighborhood, and personal divisions may be played out through children. . . . Political or religious allegiance, misguided desire for purity and order, the sheer lust to see one's children privileged, all may fuel a violence otherwise too crude to tolerate. The repulsive, contorted faces of white mothers shouting at black children seeking to enter schoolrooms may haunt most women. But they are faces of maternal practice and represent a temptation to which mothers are liable—self-righteous violence against the outsider. (Ruddick 1983b, 244)

It is true that a great deal of the violence mothers use or endorse is based on the hatred of outsiders who do not really threaten their children. But some threats to children from outsiders are real, and thus preservative love may require a violent response to protect them. Thus a mother's commitment to her own children does not necessarily imply a commitment to pacifism.

Ruddick's second argument is based on a distinction between abstract and concrete styles of thinking. Ruddick defines these thinking styles as follows:

> Abstraction refers to a cluster of interrelated dispositions to simplify, dissociate, generalize and sharply define. Its opposition, which I call "concreteness," respects complexity, connection, particularity and ambiguity. (Ruddick 1983b, 249)

According to Ruddick, maternal thinking is concrete while military thinking is abstract. Maternal practice requires a realistic awareness of and attention to a child's particular features. In contrast, rationalizing warfare requires that we simplify (or oversimplify) complex and ambiguous situations. In Chapter 4 I argued that morality requires both concrete attention to the particularities of a situation *and* guiding principles or priorities. Although Ruddick emphasizes the need for concreteness, maternal practice as she describes it also incorporates the general priorities of the preservation, growth, and acceptability of one's children. However, the abstract style of thinking she associates with warfare appeals to abstractions as a means of diverting attention from the concrete realities of the lives affected by one's actions. For instance, the abstract principle of "freedom" has been used to rationalize and distract from all kinds of actions which from a concrete perspective are clearly moral atrocities. Thus, as I will explore further later, the important difference between practices is not whether they incorporate abstract principles, but whether they do so cynically or responsibly, in ways that obscure or illuminate context. The abstract thinking Ruddick criticizes is cynical or rides roughshod over context.

Ruddick believes that the connections between these practices and their styles of thinking are so close that each style of thinking *promotes* certain practices: Concrete thinking promotes peacemaking and abstract thinking promotes warmaking. She writes:

> Abstraction and the morality to which it is conducive are warlike. Willing warriors are loyal to abstract causes and abstract states. They are encouraged an "abstract hatred of the enemy" that will allow them to kill. They invent weapons and pray for victories whose victims most of them would not be willing to imagine. (Ruddick 1983b, 250)

In contrast, Ruddick argues that the concrete style of maternal thinking challenges the rationalizations for warfare. Through concrete thinking, "we see that we are shooting at conscripts, who are young, often poor, boys . . . we look at the homes where the bombs fall" (Ruddick 1983b, 251). An awareness of the concrete effects of violence will not allow us to tolerate violence, and should lead us to make a commitment to pacifism.

I challenge the claim that concrete thinking promotes pacifism and that abstract thinking promotes warfare. I will do so by comparing the three general philosophical approaches to questions of war and peace: realism, just war theory, and pacifism. "Realists" argue that war is outside the realm of morality and can only be evaluated in terms of its effectiveness in promoting a state's interests. Because war is by nature amoral, questions about whether a particular war is justified or whether it is waged in a just manner are irrelevant. By simplifying and generalizing about war in a way that makes attention to a war's concrete features irrelevant, realists are obviously guilty of the kind of abstraction Ruddick criticizes, and this abstraction is unquestionably conducive to warfare.

But Ruddick is opposed not only to realism, but to "just war" theory as well. Just war theorists, such as Michael Walzer (1977), argue that there are just and unjust reasons for war, and just and unjust ways of waging war, and they try to distinguish between them. For instance, just war theorists make a moral distinction between wars motivated by self-preservative defense and wars motivated by the desire to spread one's religious beliefs. Likewise, within war they distinguish between the killing of combatants and the killing of civilians. Ruddick regards these distinctions as dangerous abstractions:

> In distinguishing between permitted and forbidden acts of war, just-war theories actually give us the conceptual tools to justify any war. They do so partly by inventing a language that encourages us to turn away from the details of suffering, to see instead the just causes and conventional rules of war. Good is distinguished from evil, soldier from civilian, war from peace .. . . Although a civilizing presence when compared to amoral militarism, just-war theory is an exercise in abstraction. (Ruddick 1983b, 250–1)

In other words, the abstractions just war theorists use allow them to tolerate violence, and by tolerating any violence we begin down a slippery slope that allows us to tolerate more and more violence. According to Ruddick, despite their differences, both realism and just war theory rely on abstraction in a way that promotes warfare.

The problem is that pacifism, at least as it is usually understood, is an *abstract* commitment; it is the renunciation of violence *regardless* of context. In fact, pacifism is like realism in its refusal to make moral distinctions about the reasons for warfare or the conduct of war. For pacifists, all war and all violence is immoral, and making moral distinctions between different wars or acts of violence is itself dangerous. That is, they find war so horrifying that they refuse to look at it concretely. Although Ruddick criticizes just war theory for appealing to abstractions like "soldier" and "civilian," her approach is actually *more*, not less, abstract than just war theory when it refuses to recognize such distinctions. So Ruddick is mistaken in her claim that the concreteness of maternal thinking implies pacifism. By its very nature, a concrete style of thinking *rules out* the abstract renunciation of violence.

It is because of its appeal to abstractions that pacifism is an inadequate moral theory. The abstract commitment to nonviolence, with its refusal to separate means from ends, means that no evil is great enough to justify a violent response. Of course, pacifists respond to aggression, but in nonviolent ways. Unfortunately, however, nonviolent forms of resistance do not always work. They attempt to appeal to the conscience of one's aggressors, but aggressors do not always share the resisters' moral convictions. Indeed, this may be part of what makes them aggressors in the first place. Walzer notes that the only impression nonviolent resistance "seems to have made on Hitler was to excite his impulse to trample on what, to his mind, was contemptible weakness" (Walzer 1977, 333). Paradoxically then, the abstract renunciation of violence requires a willingness to accept violence toward oneself. The extent of this paradox is evident in Gandhi's advice to the Jews of Germany that they should commit suicide rather than fight back against Nazi tyranny. As Walzer writes, "Here nonviolence, under extreme conditions, collapses into violence directed at oneself rather than at one's murderers, though why it should take that direction I cannot understand" (Walzer 1977, 332).

In its acceptance of violence toward the self, pacifism mirrors the second level of the ethic of care, in which one's commitment to care for others comes at the expense of care for oneself. One form of abstraction is simplification, and pacifism simplifies by recognizing only one basic principle, just as the conventional level of the ethic of care simplifies by recognizing only one basic principle. In both cases these principles dictate one's obligations toward others while ignoring one's obligations toward oneself. But just as the commitment to care for others should not mean ignoring one's own needs, the commitment to nonviolence should not require surrendering to violence toward oneself. In each case a more adequate approach requires a second principle recognizing the equality of the self to the other, and requires attempting to balance one's obligations to self and others. It also requires recognizing the complexity of moral situations: At times the two principles cannot be reconciled. In fact, an approach which seeks to balance one's commitment to nonviolence and one's commitment to one's own life and well-being is not only fairer to oneself, but may even deter violence. As Davion points out, "In at least some situations, showing a willingness to use violence can actually prevent an attack. Many women report that standing in a fighting stance and yelling 'no' intimidates rapists" (Davion 1990, 93).

Jean Grimshaw makes a distinction between principles and rules that is helpful in this context. "A rule specifies or forbids a certain sort of action, and to follow a rule is to accept a guideline for one's conduct whose purpose is to eliminate the need for reflection" (Grimshaw 1986, 207). "Violence is always wrong" would be an example of a rule. While applying this rule would require a certain amount of reflection on what constitutes violence, this rule does not direct our attention to contextual particularities and thus has the effect of discouraging reflection. However, principles merely identify certain priorities that we should keep in mind in reaching a moral decision. Examples of principles are: "Consider whether your action will harm others" and "Consider whether you are being fair to yourself." Thus principles, in contrast to rules, invite us to pay close attention to the complexities of a particular situation. A *rule* of nonviolence cannot arise out of a (mature) ethic of care as expressed in maternal thinking. However, a mature ethic of care might include a *principle* of nonviolence.

So far I have assumed that the pacifism Ruddick endorses is the standard form of pacifism which expresses a rule of nonviolence. However, given that Ruddick defined pacifism as a *commitment* to nonviolence rather than as an absolute renunciation of violence, perhaps her pacifism is best understood as expressing a principle rather than a rule of nonviolence. In fact, Ruddick criticizes pacifists who make an abstract renunciation of violence, and suggests that pacifists learn from maternal practice to attend to the battle at hand (Ruddick 1983b, 252). While Victoria Davion insists that Ruddick is inadvertently defending the *opposite* of pacifism, Ruddick wants to distinguish between different kinds of pacifism. In a later work, she calls them "absolute" and "contextual" pacifism, where contextual pacifists

> train for nonviolent resistance and look critically at every call to violence, but they refuse to rule out in advance an exceptional circumstance . . . in which they would use violence to disarm and dislodge attackers or oppressors even if that meant killing them. (Ruddick 1992, 1300)

Ruddick's "contextual pacifism" suggests that violence generally, but not necessarily, contradicts the purposes of the ethic of care, and thus that violence should be an important consideration in moral decisionmaking.

Maternal or care-based defenses of absolute pacifism accept an overly simplistic version of the ethic of care that unnecessarily and unhelpfully opposes it to justice. However, what Ruddick calls contextual pacifism shares with (at least certain versions of) just war theory a concrete perspective on war and violence. They differ only in their background assumptions about the effectiveness of nonviolent resistance and the necessity for violent response. For instance, Walzer devotes only a few pages of his book to pacifism, dismissing it by citing instances in which nonviolent resistance has failed to deter aggression. In contrast, Ruddick argues that the effectiveness of war is routinely overestimated, while the successes of nonviolent actions have been underreported and minimized (Ruddick 1992, 1301). However, this difference in assumptions can be overcome: Just as contextual pacifism improves upon absolute pacifism, a just war theory committed to finding nonviolent strategies would improve upon one which regards nonviolent strategies as largely useless.

In this section I have argued that the ethic of care does not imply pacifism, as least as pacifism is conventionally understood. This is because "abstract" pacifism entails a *rule* of nonviolence. However, the ethic of care may imply a *principle* of nonviolence which must be balanced against other, sometimes conflicting, principles. In general, the ethic of care's contextuality does not allow us to derive any specific rules, but its priorities allow us to articulate general principles the application of which requires close attention to context.

Elder-Care and Welfare

A second possible public application of an ethic of care is the publicly funded support provided by the welfare state. This support can take many different forms, ranging from general assistance programs for those most desperately in need to universal programs such as national health care. In order to limit my discussion, I will focus on programs providing long-term care for the disabled elderly. However, much of what I will say also applies to publicly funded care for children or for non-elderly disabled people. After clarifying in what sense such programs can be understood as applications of the ethic of care, I will evaluate publicly funded elder-care in light of the criticism that such care is a not a public, but a private responsibility, and that making it a public responsibility undermines the ethic of care in its private context. In response, I will defend the opposite position: Recognizing elder-care as a public responsibility actually *promotes* the ethic of care in family relationships. As I will show, the stark difference between these two positions results from their opposing accounts of the ethic of care. Finally, I will discuss welfare programs more generally in showing that the ethic of care's relational approach is superior to the ethic of justice's typically individualistic approach.

Before I go further, I need to make clear what I mean by long-term care for the disabled elderly, and to show why, on the surface, it would seem to be a public responsibility. There are many elderly people who have no acute medical problems but whose quality of life is dependent upon long-term care. With the help of personal care and social-support services, they are often able to maintain independent living arrangements, which the vast majority of elderly people desire. However, because they cannot find or finance this long-term care, millions of elderly people who with some help could live on their own are forced to become institutionalized or move in with family members. Nursing home placements are not only premature in many cases, but are either financially burdensome (for families who can afford them) or difficult to find (for Medicaid recipients). Also, nursing homes often do not provide the rehabilitative kind of care elderly people need in order to lead a meaningful life. Elderly people who depend on their families for long-term care usually depend *exclusively* on their families. In 1988, Norman Daniels wrote that families provided about 80 percent of all home health care to the partially disabled elderly. This puts a tremendous strain on the family caregivers, who are usually women, and the resulting family tensions often diminish the level of care given to the elderly.

Even when families willingly assume the responsibility of taking care of their elderly members, they need relief from this responsibility. For instance, both caregivers and recipients of care benefit from day-care centers for the elderly. When I refer to long-term care for the elderly, I will mean any of these services, including personal-care services, social services, nursing care, and rehabilitative therapy, which are designed to give partially disabled elderly people the most autonomous lifestyle possible. The services I will discuss are publicly funded, and may be institutionally or home-based.[1]

I must first establish whether and in what sense publicly funded elder-care is an application of the ethic of care. For the most part, such a program seems to provide a clear example of a traditionally private ethic of care made public. That is, traditionally, most elder-care has been provided by and financially supported by family members. In contrast, the elder-care I will consider is public in that it is provided by professional, publicly funded careworkers. Thus in contrast to the maternal pacifism I discussed earlier, here there is no need to establish that a particular private activity implies *a different* public activity. Here the public and private activities are, to the greatest extent possible, *the same* activity. Long-term care provided by paid careworkers *replaces* and seeks to approximate as closely as possible long-term care provided by family members, or at least an ideal version of that care. To the extent that it does, there seems to be little question that publicly-funded elder-care should be considered a version of the ethic of care.

However, the potential generality of such an elder-care program raises questions about whether it is a version of the ethic of care. If such a program were generalized in the sense that it were available to all elderly people, regardless of individual differences of wealth, it might be argued that the program is not an application of the ethic of care but an application of the ethic of justice to what was traditionally regarded as a matter of care. In fact, the tensions between the two ethics raise important questions about whether publicly funded elder-care should be distributed generally or by need, and I will not answer these questions here. Instead I will assume that the program considered here is need-based, and thus that it clearly reflects a version of the ethic of care.

Critics have appealed to alternative conceptions of the ethic of care to argue that elder-care is not a public responsibility. They state that elder-care is a filial obligation, one of many "family values" that have recently begun to deteriorate. (Wolfe 1989). They argue that publicly funded elder-care not only does nothing to promote private responsibilities but by sending the message that one is not expected to take care of one's elderly parents, it actually contributes to the breakdown of such responsibilities. Thus such advocates of "family values" argue that in order to strengthen the family, we should privatize responsibility for care of the elderly. During the 1980s, they tried to do so in the United States by proposing Family Responsibility Laws in about half the states. These bills sought to require family members to reimburse the state for their relatives' long-term care, which is currently paid by Medicaid. If family members could not afford to do so, they would be forced to provide the needed care themselves, which was considered the preferred option in any case. Although these laws were defended in economic terms, the underlying justification of Family Responsibility Laws was the promotion of filial obligations in particular and "family values" in general.

Those who take this approach regard publicly funded elder-care as just one part of a welfare state which needs to be dismantled in the interest of personal responsibility and family values. For instance, Sir Keith Joseph describes the objectives of the Tory approach as follows: "to strengthen the family, thrift and social reliance; to remove crutches from those who can walk; to strengthen the social network" (Goodin 1988, 343–4). Similarly, a recent Australian minister for social services writes:

> My personal preference would be to see a higher level of personal independence and family interdependence . . . with young people living at home and receiving support from their families, with husbands and wives recognizing their obligations of mutual support, with families committing themselves to the care of their aged members and parents accepting their primary responsibility for the care of their own children. (Goodin 1988, 344)

Such advocates of "family values" believe that the welfare state threatens these goals by allowing people to rely on the state rather than on their families. They believe, in short, that this public application of the ethic of care *undermines* its corresponding private ethic of care. It might be argued that such critics are insincere when they defend their opposition to the welfare state on the grounds of "family values," or what I am calling a private ethic of care. Perhaps their ultimate commitment is to an economic program that is in their own self-interest, as it absolves them of any responsibility for the well-being of those outside their own families. But I will take them at their word and assume that they are committed to good family relationships and that they believe that publicly funded elder-care, along with other welfare programs, is detrimental to such relationships.

I want to challenge this argument by examining the version of the ethic of care that is implicit in what it considers "good family relationships." I will argue that the privatization of elder-care promotes a version of the ethic of care which is inconsistent with the autonomy of both its providers and its recipients. In other words, these advocates of "family values" defend what I have called distorted care. As I argued in Chapter 2, care is distorted when its provider is denied autonomy and/or when it does not promote its recipient's autonomy. In contrast, I seek to promote what I have called genuine care, or care which both arises out of and promotes personal autonomy. I will show that by recognizing elder-care as a public responsibility we promote genuine care.

First, I will consider the effects on family care providers of the elimination of publicly funded elder-care. These caregivers are usually women, and the immediate effect on them is that they are generally forced out of the paid workplace in order to care for elderly relatives. This in turn undermines the autonomy they could gain through paid employment, so they become increasingly dependent on other family members. As Daniels writes:

> "Family care" policies typically require some (typically female) members of the family to abandon paid employment to care for needy relatives; and by abandoning paid employment, they compromise their capacity, economically, to take care of themselves. (Daniels 1988, 348)

The fact that privatizing responsibility for elder-care undermines women's autonomy suggests that shifting the responsibility for care work to public sources would promote gender equality.

However, those defending privatized elder-care on the basis of "family values" do not regard women's inequality as an undesirable consequence of their approach. In fact, their arguments are really an appeal to the "traditional" family structure, in which men are public breadwinners and women are private caretakers. From this perspective women's increasing participation in the paid workplace, and the publicly funded elder-care that helps make it possible, are part of the problem. Requiring families to take responsibility for the care of their elderly members will help restore the traditional family structure. In their view we can promote the ethic of care by eliminating the autonomy of its providers. That is, if women do not want to spend their lives as caregivers, we could respond by redistributing caregiving responsibilities among various family members and paid caregivers, *or* we could respond by eliminating all other options so that they will do so anyway. The family values account chooses the latter option.

The "family values" criticism of publicly funded elder-care not only threatens the autonomy of caregivers but it actually undermines the motivations they *do* have to take care of their elderly relatives. Many people do feel filial obligations but, without any assistance, they find that these obligations are overwhelming. Incidentally, these obligations are actually *more* overwhelming now than they were in the "good old days" that the advocates of family values hold up as an ideal. Compared to a century ago, we now have many more frail elderly people needing long-term care and needing it for longer. Because elder-care responsibilities are so overwhelming,

> Some who would provide care, or would do so for longer periods, are unable to meet the responsibilities they feel because appropriate support services are not available. This leads to frustration, guilt, and even rationalization that can undermine an individual's conviction that he or she has such family responsibilities. (Daniels 1988, 115)

Thus publicly funded elder-care should not be seen as a mere substitute for, or as a deterrent to family-provided elder-care. By providing day-care facilities, social-support services, and at-home medical and personal-care assistance, we lighten the burden on family caregivers. This allows and encourages them to carry out whatever responsibilities they do feel. The public ethic of care supports rather than undermines its corresponding private ethic of care.

Of course, some sons and daughters feel no responsibility or inclination to provide care for their elderly parents, and will not be encouraged to do so by the public provision of elder-care. However, this is certainly no reason to eliminate publicly funded elder-care. As Robert Goodin writes:

> It is certainly true that there are certain sorts of affective support that only the family can provide. But if the families are unwilling to provide such support, it will do no good to try to compel it. Although we might be able to extract the material component, the affective component will still be missing. (Goodin 1988, 347)

Another way of putting this is that while we may be able to coerce distorted care, we cannot coerce genuine care. Rather than promoting good family relationships, such coercion would be likely to intensify conflict within the family and threaten the well-being of the vulnerable elderly person. Thus in trying to enforce filial obligations, we are being unfair not only to the caregiver, but to the recipient of care.

Next I will consider the effects of the elimination of publicly funded elder-care on the elderly who need care. Eliminating such care would mean, first of all, that the elderly would be dependent upon their families (or others who volunteered) for this care. According to the "family values" position, this is a good thing:

Dependency upon one's family, understood as an expression of family commitment, is morally preferable to dependency upon the state, understood as a result of the breakdown of family commitment. Yet most elderly people disagree. They wish to avoid being dependent on their families, expressing a near universal preference for public over private sources of assistance (Goodin 1988, 352). This preference for public over private support does not mean that the elderly do not value family commitment, but that they seek genuine rather than distorted care.

Publicly provided support allows for its recipients' autonomy in a way that privately provided support does not. As Goodin explains, public and private sources of support differ with regard to discretion: "families must have substantial discretion; public officials may, by law, be deprived of it" (Goodin 1988, 352). That is, family provided care is necessarily voluntary, whereas state-provided care can be understood as an entitlement which must be honored. This difference is obviously important to the recipients of care, and helps explain the preference of elderly people for public rather than private support. Goodin writes, "Those who depend upon particular others for satisfaction of their basic needs are rendered, by that dependency, susceptible to exploitation by those upon whom they depend" (Goodin 1988, 121). Whether or not caregivers choose to exploit those they care for, the recipients of such care cannot be described as autonomous.

If recipients have an enforceable right to the care they receive, their dependency need not threaten their autonomy. For this reason it is crucial that state officials not be given the discretion individual families have had over the support elderly people receive. Although they must exercise a certain degree of discretion in deciding whether a specific case falls under a general rule governing entitlements, state officials may have their discretion minimized by being put under strong legal obligations to provide support (Goodin 1988, 352–3). By limiting discretion in this way, we recognize this support as a right rather than as a form of charity. As I have shown in Chapter 4, the ethic of care and the ethic of justice can both endorse the idea that care is sometimes a right.

I have shown that publicly funded elder-care does not threaten, but promotes an ethic of care that values autonomy. In assuming that removing options strengthens care, and that introducing options threatens care, the argument against publicly funded elder-care is like many other "family values" positions. For instance, abortion parental consent laws are defended on the grounds that parents and children *should* communicate with each other about sex and birth control. Proponents seem to believe that by removing all other (legal) options, we can force parents and children to communicate with one another. In fact, at best we can force a distorted form of communication, and at worst we force pregnant girls to consider potentially tragic options like illegal abortions. We cannot coerce people to enact a genuine ethic of care. We can only support their own efforts to do so by promoting their autonomy. Understanding elder-care as a public responsibility helps do this.

Finally, I will consider questions about the relationship between this version of the ethic of care and the ethic of justice. I have argued that the two ethics need not be understood as mutually exclusive, but are both necessary for an adequate morality. Different versions of the ethic of justice take opposing views on the welfare state, and I have suggested that we use the ethic of care as a criterion in deciding among them. Let me address the view that an ethic of justice alone would suffice in defending the welfare state. After all, those who defend the welfare state generally do so by appealing to an ethic of justice, not an ethic of care. It would seem then, that either standard justice-based defenses of the welfare state must be inadequate in some way *or* the ethic of care is unnecessary in defending the welfare state. In what follows, I will settle this dilemma by showing that standard justice-based defenses of the welfare state are indeed inadequate, and that a social conception of the self, such as that embedded in the ethic of care, is essential in defending a desirable form of the welfare state. An ethic of justice could adopt such a conception of the self, but in doing so it would depart from standard versions of that ethic by bringing to the foreground concerns that are typically left in the background.

The standard ways of looking at the welfare state can be understood in terms of the equality-difference debate.[2] Simply stated, the problem addressed by this debate is: How does one equally treat people who have been identified as different? I will outline the two leading attempts to define equality in the context of difference. According to the first approach, which is often called the "equal treatment" approach, the problem is that people have been categorized as different when they are not different in any morally relevant way. In general, the equal treatment approach is suspicious of claims that any group of people is "different," because the false claim of difference has been used so often to rationalize unjust discrimination. Although conceding that some people are in fact different in a way that requires special treatment, this approach holds that equality requires integrating as many people as possible into the social mainstream.

However, according to the second approach, which is often called the "special treatment" approach, equality requires that we not deny or ignore the real differences between people, but that we acknowledge and accommodate those differences. Behind this approach is the recognition that treating everyone equally in an institution designed with only certain people in mind can harm those whose lives differ from the people for whom the institutions were designed. In a context of inequality, equal treatment can perpetuate inequalities. However, as equal treatment advocates point out, special treatment does the same thing: Identifying people as different and in need of special accommodations contributes to their stigmatization and thus to their inequality.

The two leading justice positions on the welfare state can be understood as versions of the "equal treatment" and "special treatment" approaches. The "different" people in question are those who do not seem to be self-sufficient, who seem to need public support of some kind. Those taking the equal treatment approach criticize welfare programs on the grounds that in fact such people are not really different from the rest of us; they can become self-sufficient or at least rely on their families for support. Conversely, those taking the special treatment approach defend welfare programs on the grounds that such people are in fact different in that they, unlike the rest of us, are unable to take care of themselves or rely on private forms of support and therefore need public support. Thus if one begins with the individualistic assumption that "normal" people are self-sufficient, defending welfare programs requires that one label welfare recipients "different." For instance, as Tronto points out, in Goodin's defense of welfare he seems to identify himself and other moral philosophers with the protectors, and to think of the vulnerable as "other." (Tronto 1993, 209)

There are two kinds of problems with labeling welfare recipients different on the grounds that they are not self-sufficient. First, this claim of difference is simply false. In fact, no one is self-sufficient; we all depend on particular others and social institutions for our physical and psychological well-being. Second, in making the false claim that "normal" people are self-sufficient, we perpetuate conventional versions of the ethic of care that I have shown to be inadequate. As I have already noted in discussing the "family values" position, the assumption that "normal" people are self-sufficient applies only to the public sphere. In fact, this assumption accepts, and even encourages, dependency in the private sphere. Those with roles in the public sphere are considered self-sufficient only because the care work that is done for them in the private sphere is taken for granted, and thus devalued. In this way the assumption that welfare recipients are different in virtue of their neediness reinforces the traditional public/private dichotomy, and the conventional boundaries of care and justice. It also promotes a paternalistic form of care that threatens the autonomy of care recipients; when welfare recipients are labeled different, caregivers and policy makers are likely to assume that they are incompetent and thus unable to determine their own needs.

I have shown that standard versions of the ethic of justice are inadequate for defending welfare policy because of their individualism. Now I will consider how one might approach welfare policy if one begins with a social conception of the self. This approach would begin with a public discussion of needs, which, as Tronto points out, are intersubjective and contestable in a way that interests are not. She writes:

> A society that took caring seriously would engage in a discussion of the issues of public life from a vision not of autonomous, equal, rational actors each pursuing separate ends, but from a vision of interdependent actors, each of whom needs and provides care in a variety of ways and each of whom has other interests and pursuits that exist outside the realm of care. (Tronto 1993, 168)

Focusing on relationships between individuals rather than on the boundaries around individuals has several clear implications. First, it reveals that it is not enough to ask who deserves how much of what, as individualistic approaches are likely to do. We must also pay close attention to the quality of relationships between the people involved. For this reason I have evaluated publicly funded elder-care and its "family values" critique based on whether each proposal promotes healthy relationships between caregivers and care recipients.

There are many situations in which this relational approach allows us to escape the problems faced by the traditional approaches. For instance, children whose families cannot afford to pay for school lunches are harmed both by the equal treatment approach of ignoring their "difference" and letting them go hungry, and by the special treatment approach of providing a free lunch program for those identified, and thereby stigmatized, as poor. In contrast, paying attention to the relationships between the poor children and their classmates might suggest that we provide a free lunch program to *all* students (Minow 1990, 96). That is, it is not merely important *whether* poor children are provided a free lunch at school, but *how* a free lunch program is implemented: Does it isolate and stigmatize children from poor families, or does it allow for positive relations between children from different backgrounds?

A relational approach also challenges the equality-difference dilemma by revealing that difference is a property of a relationship, not of an individual. No individuals are intrinsically different; individuals are different only in relation to others. Moreover, differences are not neutral comparisons but implicit devaluations of the "different" individual for deviating from the norm. Thus, in assessing welfare policy, we need to pay attention not only to personal relationships between individuals but also to relationships between the groups who give and receive care, or those labeled "normal" and those labeled "different." Martha Minow suggests this when she explains why "expressions of empathy, altruism, or an ethos of care toward the 'different person'" are inadequate:

> Those impulses may be helpful, but they fundamentally preserve the pattern of relationships in which some people enjoy the power and position from which to consider—as a gift or act of benevolence—the needs of others without having to encounter their own implication in the social patterns that assign the problem to those others. (Minow 1990, 219)

Among these social patterns is the way "caregivers" and "care recipients" are often seen and treated as separate and distinct groups, such that caregivers, understood to include policy makers, welfare professionals, and people of their social class, only give care, while welfare recipients only receive care. According to this approach welfare recipients are the problem because they only receive care.

In fact, however, these caregivers are also care recipients, and these care recipients are also caregivers. The supposed caregiver class is also the one that can afford to have a wife at home and/or maids, nurses, nannies (or other paid child care). They are generally able and apt to hire all sorts of services and labor to take care of all sorts of personal needs (and luxuries). The difference between them and those who rely on welfare is that the "self-sufficient" have the resources to purchase such care for self or family. And from whom? Very often the maids, nannies, nurses, child care workers, etc. who provide the care are drawn from the same social group as those on welfare. If not, they certainly are often those closest to falling into such need due to economic changes, medical costs, and the like. In other words, when they are among the employed, members of this group are frequently employed in serving and taking care of the needs of the group that considers itself self-sufficient. Even when that care is not provided to the better off, a great many welfare recipients are providing child care to their own children. The problem is not that welfare recipients only receive care, but that the care that they provide is not usually recognized as valuable.

Thus a defense of welfare policy that pays close attention to the relationships between care providers and care recipients is superior to one that labels welfare recipients as different. This attention to relationships reveals that the members of the two groups are equal in that they are dependent upon others for care. It also reveals that there is a relationship of power between these two groups based on the fact that we recognize and value only certain forms of caregiving. In order to make the care provided by the welfare state compatible with the autonomy of its recipients, we must challenge this power relationship. This in turn requires that we take caregiving, in all its forms, more seriously.

Conclusion

In this chapter I have examined two possible public applications of the ethic of care. In each case I have asked whether the proposal is a version of the ethic of care, what the value of that version of the ethic of care is, and the relationship between that version of the ethic of care and the ethic of justice.

I have shown a standard form of pacifism has problems in all three areas. It does not express the ethic of care, at least in its most developed form. Pacifism does not arise from the contextuality of the ethic of care, and more generally, a contextual approach cannot give rise to *any* specific rules. The absolute renunciation of violence reflects a conventional level of the ethic of care, at which the commitment to others requires that one sacrifice oneself. However, the contextual pacifism Ruddick defends avoids these problems. It also reveals that the dichotomy between pacifism and just-war theory breaks down, and that these care and justice approaches are at their best when they are integrated.

In the second case I have shown that certain welfare programs succeed in all three areas. I have shown that publicly funded elder-care expresses a version of the ethic of care that is informed by a concern for the autonomy of both care providers and care recipients. That is, it promotes genuine rather than distorted care. I have also shown that the ethic of care is needed for a satisfactory welfare policy because its social conception of the self helps us resolve problems of equality and difference that are intractable if we are committed to the individual-istic conception of the self in the ideal type of the ethic of justice.

I have considered only two of many different proposed versions of the ethic of care. However, in my examination of these two proposals according to these three questions, I have offered a model of how one might evaluate any proposed public version of the ethic of care.

Notes

1. This account of long-term care for the elderly comes from Daniels (1988).

2. Besides the welfare state, the equality-difference debate addresses many other ques-tions concerning discrimination and accommodation. Although I will not pursue these here, I believe the ethic of care has important implications in these contexts as well. Some of these are explored in Minow (1990).

6

The Moral Significance of the Care/Justice Debate

▼

Much of this book has been an overview of the recent discussions and debates about the ethic of care and its relationship to the ethic of justice. In the past decade the ethic of care and the ethic of justice have received an enormous amount of attention. Some would probably say that these areas have received *too much* attention. Susan Moller Okin writes that *"Unfortunately,* much feminist intellectual energy in the 1980s has gone into the claim that 'justice' and 'rights' are masculinist ways of thinking about morality that feminists should eschew or radically revise, advocating a morality of care" (Okin 1989, 15; my emphasis). In this chapter I will show that the care/justice debate has been morally significant. However, while many commentators have viewed the debate as a contest between the ethic of justice and the ethic of care, and have tried to establish the superiority of one of the ethics, the debate has not settled the question of which ethic is superior. Instead, its significance, I believe, lies in the fact that it has established that care and justice should not be seen as competitors, but as allies which are indispensable to one another in our attempts to create a world more conducive to human well-being.

This chapter is divided into two sections, each of which demonstrates some of the specific moral implications of the care/justice debate in general and of this work in particular. In the first section I will discuss the lessons revealed by examination of the ideal types of care and justice. Specifically, there are dangers associated with the ideal types of both ethics, especially for women. Yet the interaction of the two ethics allows us to move beyond the ideal types to positive versions of the ethics. In the second section I will examine the relationship between the resulting versions of the two ethics. I will show that it is a mistake to regard either justice or care as morally primary, as they are mutually interdependent. Also, despite the fact that the best versions of the ethics often converge in the sense that they reach the same or compatible conclusions, they remain distinct ethics, each with its own ontology, method, and priorities.

▼

Finally, I will propose that we understand the ethics as integrated in the sense that they should both be used in any moral situation.

Beyond the Ideal Types

Prior to the care/justice debate, moral philosophy was dominated by the approach I have called the ethic of justice. That is, moral philosophy tended to focus on general principles rather than attention to contextual detail, on the self as an independent individual rather than the self in relation to others, and on varying commitments to equality rather than commitments to maintaining relationships. When the ethic of justice is not balanced by the ethic of care, it tends to take on exaggerated, distorted forms by focusing on only one of two interrelated sets of features. I have examined some of these exaggerations in this book. Here I will review these and cite some other ways in which the exclusive focus on justice considerations has distorted moral theory. Again, I do not mean to suggest that all versions of the ethic of justice are guilty of the following distortions, but that these distortions tend to arise with the exclusive focus on justice considerations and neglect of care considerations.

As I have shown, the individualistic focus of the ethic of justice has led to an excessively psychological account of autonomy, ignoring the social conditions necessary for self-determination. The ethic of justice also tends to understand moral knowledge as an individual achievement, such that rational reflection allows one to achieve moral knowledge. The ethic of care's emphasis on social interdependency leads to a different perspective on moral knowledge. It emphasizes that our moral knowledge, and the rational capacity to achieve it, is ultimately dependent on the education we have received from parents, teachers, etc. Most moral philosophers have not only overlooked the importance of moral education but in so doing have trivialized women's traditional role as moral educators. The emphasis on individual rationality is troubling in another way as well: It promotes the mistaken view that moral knowledge is *guaranteed* by individual rationality. In fact, moral knowledge depends not only on rationality but on socially determined factors, such as information, as well. As Cheshire Calhoun explains, "Our being motivated to raise questions of justification in the first place and our ability to address those questions once raised depends at least partially on the social availability of moral criticisms and of morally relevant information" (Calhoun 1988, 457). Thus the ethic of care's emphasis on the social determinants of moral knowledge addresses limitations in the ethic of justice's emphasis on the individual reflection required for moral knowledge.

I have shown that the ethic of justice has also made the mistake of assuming that our interests can always be understood individualistically. This assumption leads to the view that the goods of a group are nothing but the goods of the individual members of that group. But the shared goods of relationships cannot be reduced to individual benefits and burdens. As Virginia Held writes,

> Consider the difference between playing music as an expression of individual achievement and playing music as a social, shared activity. . . . While we may hesitate to subscribe to any general claim that shared aesthetic experiences are always or even in general to be preferred to individual ones, it does seem that social arrangements which foster interpersonal, intergroup, and intercultural aesthetic experiences may be worth striving for, and that they cannot be evaluated in terms that measure only the development of expressive monads. (Held 1993, 185–6)

Combined with the priority of equality, this individualism has led to the illusion that a society of equals would be an ideal one. The introduction of care considerations provides a check against such illusions by reminding us of another important dimension of the good life: human relationships.

The individualism of the ethic of justice also seems to undermine its moral effectiveness. By understanding interests purely individualistically, the ethic of justice is able to motivate actions in the interests of others only by requiring that one sacrifice one's own self-interest, something that is notoriously difficult to do. In contrast, the ethic of care's emphasis on the social constitution of the self allows us to understand the extent to which our interests are inseparable from those of others, and thus to find integrative solutions, or ways of acting that promote the shared interests of self and other. Thus the individualism of the ethic of justice means that it requires a strength of will over one's inclinations that the ethic of care does not, making the ethic of justice less reliable in motivating right action. (Jaggar 1995, 12)

The abstract emphasis of the ethic of justice has led to other distortions. As I have shown, it has promoted the mistaken view that general principles are sufficient to resolve moral conflicts, when in fact general principles often conflict with one another in a way that cannot be resolved by a still more general principle. The emphasis on abstraction has also led to the view that the more abstract moral reasoning is, the better it is. It promotes the idea that disconnecting ourselves from particular others is necessary to morality and that emotional involvement is detrimental to morality. Not only does this completely disregard the moral experiences of most women and the ethic of care's recognition that emotional responsiveness is essential to morality, but it also renders the ethic of justice ineffective. Abstract principles can only be put into effect if individuals are willing to pay attention to and care about the situations that call for them. It seems likely that our moral failures today come not from lacking strong enough moral principles to address the moral situations before us, but from our refusal to face those situations. As Joan Tronto writes, "Ironically, it is precisely the strength of universal moral theory, its detachment from the world, that makes it inadequate to solve the kinds of moral problems that now present themselves. . . . From such a point of view we cannot explain how 'attentiveness' can be a central moral concern" (Tronto 1993, 152–3).

By emphasizing elements previously ignored by moral philosophy, the ethic of care protects against these sorts of extremes. Advocates of the ethic of justice claim that these focal points do not exclude the ethic of care, and they are right. But a continued emphasis on one dimension of human relationships nevertheless has the effect of prioritizing that dimension. After all, only the moral priority of the ethic of justice would explain such an exclusive focus on justice considerations (Calhoun 1988). Moreover, since the ethic of justice reflects the experiences and concerns of males (and of a particular class of males), the exclusive focus on justice is not gender-neutral. It presents the moral point of view of a small but powerful group of men as representative of humanity in general. As a result this focus serves to deny the importance of the experiences of other groups, and of women in particular. Regardless of the logical implications of standard approaches to moral philosophy, these approaches have been disparaging to the ethic of care and to women. Thus the view of moral life traditionally reflected in ethical theory is only a partial view, and attention to the ethic of care is necessary to a complete view of morality.

Much of the care/justice debate has been devoted to deciding *between* the two ethics rather than to exploring the ways in which both ethics contribute to an adequate moral perspective. This is more understandable from a care perspective than from a justice perspective. That is, given the initial prevalence of the ethic of justice, care theorists have had to devote their energies to developing and supporting the ethic of care to have it taken seriously as a distinct ethic. Such work has served to validate aspects of women's lives which have long been devalued. It has also revealed many of the implications of the ethic of care that would not have emerged from a more balanced approach, and there is certainly the need for more work in this area. However, as I have shown, there are also dangers associated with focusing on the care considerations to the exclusion of justice considerations. Doing so often leads to an ethic of care that reflects and perpetuates women's subordinate status, even though this is far from what is intended.

First, the ethic of care's social conception of the self can lead us to overlook the value of autonomy, even for caring itself. It can lead to an exaggeration of the extent to which the interests of self and other can be integrated. The ethic of care's emphasis on the particularities of situations can also direct our attention away from the general realities that structure those situations, and which require our attention for any significant change. As Alison Jaggar writes,

> Moral thinking that focuses on the specificities of a particular situation is likely to see the source of problems as lying in the personal attitudes of individual men, whites, or heterosexuals who benefit, sometimes unwittingly or unwillingly, from sexism, racism, and heterosexism, rather than in those larger institutions that give some individuals power and prestige over others. (Jaggar 1995, 20–21)

Contextuality alone is no better than abstractness alone. Moreover, the priority of maintaining relationships, when unbalanced by other priorities, can lead us to value the maintenance of relationships without regard for their quality. The ethic of care's focus on personal relations also tends to suggest that the ethic belongs in the sphere of personal relations. As I have shown, none of these distortions necessarily accompany the ethic of care; they can be overcome by including justice considerations in our moral reasoning.

In general, then, each ethic provides a check against the exaggerated, ideal type form of the other ethic. Because the ethics differ in their focal points, each is prone to its own dangers. The dangers of the ethic of care are those of traditional femininity. One danger is that care is overly self-sacrificing so that one cares for others at the expense of caring well for oneself. The second danger is that care is limited to the sphere of personal relations so that one cares for one's family members and friends, but ignores the needs of anyone outside that limited sphere. Both of these dangers are addressed by the ethic of justice. Its commitment to equality requires that one recognize oneself as of equal worth to others. The universal scope of the ethic of justice requires that we not restrict our attention to our sphere of personal relations.

There are also two main dangers in the ethic of justice, and these are the dangers of traditional masculinity. One is that individuals are understood as essentially self-sufficient, so that only negative rights are recognized, and others are owed only non-interference. The second danger is that all obligations are understood on a contractual model, or as arising out of voluntary consent. Both of these dangers are addressed by the ethic of care. Its commitment to meeting needs requires that we recognize positive rights. Likewise, the ethic of care's recognition that we have obligations to which we have not consented requires that we expand our account of obligations beyond the contractual model.

In short, the versions of care and justice I defend are ones which agree in at least two ways: by recognizing the equality of self and other, and by making their moral concern global. However, they reach these conclusions in different ways. First, the ethic of justice can recognize the equality of self and other by overcoming the tendency to give the rights and interests of others less weight than we give our own. An ethic of justice informed by care can understand that the category "human" has a substantive and not just a formal definition, and thus that humans have rights to certain basic minimal requirements without which they cannot live. In contrast, for the ethic of care the central motivational obstacle is the tendency to give the rights and interests of others *more* weight than we give our own, or self-sacrifice. Thus the ethic of care recognizes the equality of the self and other by including the self within the scope of care, or by promoting the self to equality with the other. Second, the ethic of justice can achieve global moral concern when it recognizes that one has moral obligations to which one has not consented. In contrast, the ethic of care can achieve global moral concern by recognizing that care should not be limited to personal relations.

In this section I have shown two moral implications of the care/justice debate. First, the ideal types of both the ethic of justice and the ethic of care which often underlie this debate are flawed in important ways. Used alone, either ethic tends to result in forms of moral reasoning which are both distorted and oppressive to women. Second, each of the two ethics can help us distinguish between better and worse versions of the other ethic. Such interaction between the ethics challenges their ideal types and reveals more adequate versions of the ethics which are not so diametrically opposed.

These challenges to the ideal types of justice and care raise questions about the distinctness of the two ethics. How *far* should we move beyond the ideal types? Given the fact that the ethics often agree in their conclusions, we need to ask whether the two ethics converge into a single ethic, or whether they remain distinct ethics despite the breakdown of their ideal types. In addressing this question we should remember that each of the ethics arises out of a particular ineliminable dimension of human relationships, developing a distinctive ontology, method, and set of values based on that dimension. Thus it seems likely that the ideal types of these ethics are exaggerations rather than complete illusions. Challenging the ideal types of justice and care need not mean denying that there are important differences between the two ethics. I will address this question more thoroughly in the following section when I consider various possible relationships between the ethics.

Integrating Care and Justice

Since the ideal types of care and justice break down, so too does the conventional account of their relationship to one another. However, recognizing that the conventional account of their relationship is mistaken does not immediately reveal the correct account of their relationship. Most feminist commentators would agree that both ethics are morally important, that the ethics are not as dichotomously opposed as is often thought, and that the conventional public/private boundaries of the ethics are inadequate. However, despite this agreement, there remains little agreement on the precise nature of the relationship between care and justice.

Feminist commentators have focused on two questions in examining this relationship. The first is the relative importance of the ethic of justice and the ethic of care. Both ethics may be important, but according to some, the ethic of justice has moral priority, while according to others, the ethic of care has moral priority. The second question is how similar or different the (ideal versions of the) two ethics are. According to some, the interaction of care and justice results in a convergence into a comprehensive ethic that incorporates all the features that the care/justice debate has located in two distinct ethics. Against this, others have argued that, despite their interaction, the two ethics remain independent orientations on any given situation. Here I will review and assess these views, and defend a third answer to each question. I will challenge the attempt to rank the ethics' moral priority on the grounds that they are mutually interdependent. I will argue that neither the convergence view nor the gestalt view accounts for both the distinctiveness and the interdependence of the ethics, and I will defend my own view that the two ethics can be integrated in a complete account of moral reasoning.

The view that one of the ethics is morally more basic than the other can take one of two forms, depending upon whether justice or care is regarded as basic. I will first consider the view that the ethic of justice is more basic than the ethic of care. Most often this view states that the ethic of justice concerns moral minimums, or questions of "the right." However, the ethic of care is thought to concern the realm beyond the moral minimums set by justice, or questions of "the good." Thus certain formal moral obligations set common boundaries within which we each freely define our various conceptions of the good life. Although most individuals will understand the good life to include caring relationships, caring relationships are not morally obligatory but matters of individual discretion.

This view fits well with some care theorists' insistence that the ethic of care is distorted if it is understood in terms of obligation. Joy Kroeger-Mappes (1994) points out that care is deficient if it is motivated by a sense of duty; for instance, a good parent takes care of his or her child out of love and not merely because it is the right thing to do. Moreover, while obligations can be imposed by others, we cannot be forced to care for someone; care must be freely chosen. Kroeger-Mappes concludes that "care cannot be part of any obligation theory" (Kroeger-Mappes 1994, 123). If care cannot be understood as obligatory, then it might better be classified as supererogatory, or as above and beyond the call of duty.[1] It would follow that caregivers are deserving of moral praise because they have chosen to define their lives in admirable ways, but those who choose not to be caregivers, or who even choose not to interact with other persons at all, should not be morally criticized unless these choices entail violating the moral minimums set by justice.

There are a couple of problems with the view that justice addresses questions of moral obligation, or the form of morality, while care addresses evaluative questions of the good, or the content of morality. One is that these two domains are not clearly distinct but are a matter of cultural interpretation. As Seyla Benhabib writes, "The line between matters of justice and those of the good life is not given by some moral dictionary, but evolves as a result of historical and cultural struggles" (Benhabib 1992, 75). It has been argued, for instance, that certain conceptions of the good are implicit in the purported neutrality of the liberal state. More importantly, however, even if we could reach agreement on where to draw the line between matters of the right and matters of the good, this line itself serves to prioritize matters of the right, and hence the ethic of justice, and to trivialize matters of the good, and hence the ethic of care. By holding that the ethic of justice sets the absolute moral requirements, this view suggests that the ethic of care concerns matters that are in some sense moral extras. However, the ethic of care clearly does set absolute moral requirements: A certain level of care, provided to each of us during at least certain periods of our lives, is essential to the continuance of society in general, and to a realm of justice in particular. As I have discussed, there would be no autonomous individuals without an ethic of care.

The moral importance of care suggests that we should not understand care as optional or as supererogatory but as in some sense obligatory. Although it is true that one cannot be obligated to care in the same way that one is obligated to pay taxes, this has to do with the fact that caring requires not just that one act in a certain way but that one feel a certain way, and one cannot be forced to have certain feelings. The ethic of justice is not so much a moral minimum that is in some sense *adequate* as it is as much as we can successfully *demand* of people. But none of this diminishes the necessity of caregiving, nor the fact that we *do* hold people accountable for their feelings or lack thereof. It is clear that care cannot be understood in terms of traditional obligation theory, which takes contractual obligations to be the model of moral obligations. Joan Tronto has developed a distinction between obligation and responsibility, such that responsibility is embedded in a set of implicit cultural practices, rather than in a set of formal rules or series of promises, as obligation is (Tronto 1993). But I would suggest that the contractual model of obligations is part of the ideal type of the ethic of justice that we need to move beyond.

This first account of the relationship between care and justice is certainly correct that certain minimum levels of justice are a precondition for care. A caring relationship that does not meet certain levels of fairness is morally inadequate. However, it is also the case that certain minimum levels of care are a precondition for justice, and the first account fails to recognize this. Using this line of argument, several care theorists have reversed the first view, arguing that while both of the ethics are morally important, the ethic of care is more basic than the ethic of justice. For instance, Virginia Held has argued that care is the most general and foundational moral value and that justice is an important but more narrow value within a care-based system. Care is regarded as most basic because without it there would be no life at all. As Held writes, "There has . . . been little justice within the family, but much care; so we can have care without justice. Without care, however, there would be no persons to respect, either in the public system of rights or in the family" (Held 1995, 131). Held also supports the view that care is morally more basic than justice by arguing that the ethic of care's view of persons as relational and interdependent is accurate, while the ethic of justice's view of persons as individual rights-bearers is a theoretical construct, albeit a construct which is often helpful. That is, we really *are* interdependent beings, while for certain purposes it is helpful to *think* of ourselves as independent beings. Thus the ethic of care is a more basic ethic than the ethic of justice.

While Held may be correct that a certain degree of care is necessary to mere survival in a way that justice is not, I think it is a mistake to conclude from this that care is morally a more basic ethic than justice. After all, our moral concern is with a morally adequate life and a morally adequate society, not just life itself. And while care is essential to a morally adequate life and society, so too is justice. As I have shown, the ethic of care is subject to as many distortions as is the ethic of justice, so that just as it is a mistake to think that a society governed solely by justice would be a good one, it is also a mistake to think that a society governed solely by care would be a good one. Uma Narayan makes this point with regard to the fatal neglect of female children in India: "In a nutshell, girl children are systematically and seemingly non-deliberately provided substantially less care—nutritional, medical, and so forth—than are boys" (Narayan 1995, 139). Of course, one could respond that the problem is that these girls are not cared for properly, not that they are treated unjustly. But the level of care thought appropriate for girls is itself distorted because it is not adequately informed by notions of justice. As Narayan writes, "In some families, without more justice, of a sort that changes the cultural meanings and material implications of having daughters, care will fail to be provided, and many female infants will not grow up to become adult bearers of rights" (Narayan 1995, 139). Care uninformed by justice seems as dangerous as justice uninformed by care.

I would also question Held's related claim that persons are *really* interdependent, and are only thought of as independent for certain purposes. Persons are interdependent in certain ways, but they are also independent in other ways, and it is not clear why we have to choose one as ultimately real and the other as less real. In general, it seems that it is a losing battle to try to decide which of the two ethics is *really* more basic. Whenever we find a way in which one ethic seems to be more basic than the other, we can find another way in which the other ethic is still more basic. It seems clear that *both* ethics capture something real and important about morality, and that insisting on ranking the ethics trivializes the contributions of the ethic deemed less basic. It also seems to presuppose that one of the two ethics, in its standard form, is correct, ruling out the possibility that its interaction with the other ethic might be productive.

The two accounts I have just considered focus on ways in which one of the two ethics provides a foundation for the other ethic. According to the first account, certain levels of justice are a precondition for morally adequate care, and according to the second account, an ethic of care is a precondition for an ethic of justice. In fact, both accounts are correct in these claims, and these claims do not contradict one another. It seems that there are two senses in which each of the two ethics provides a foundation for the other. In the first sense, a certain minimal level of that ethic is necessary for the very possibility of the other ethic. An ethic of justice, in which persons are treated as autonomous individuals, presupposes an ethic of care, in which dependent individuals are nurtured to autonomy. It could also be argued that in a state of complete injustice, in which one is under attack, it would be difficult if not impossible to devote the attention to others required of an ethic of care. Thus the mere existence of each of the two ethics presupposes certain basic social conditions provided by the other ethic.

In a second sense, each of the two ethics provides a foundation for the other in that each ethic provides conditions not just for the *existence* of the other ethic, but for the *moral adequacy* of it. As I showed in my discussion of the ideal types of the two ethics earlier in this chapter, each ethic helps us distinguish between better and worse versions of the other ethic. If an ethic of care endorses an action that is clearly unjust (given minimal standards of justice), then this indicates a problem with that particular version of the ethic of care. Likewise, if an ethic of justice endorses an action that is clearly uncaring, then this indicates a problem with that particular version of the ethic of justice. Also, neither the abstract emphasis of the ethic of justice nor the contextual emphasis of the ethic of care can function alone; adequate moral reasoning requires their interaction with one another.

Uma Narayan makes a related point when she argues that each ethic provides "enabling conditions" for the other ethic. For instance, an ethic of care is devoted to meeting needs, but an ethic of care cannot alone provide the conditions that will allow us to properly understand people's needs; only "serious attention to considerations of justice . . . would enable the powerless to seriously participate in the social and political discourse where such needs are contested and defined" (Narayan 1995, 139; see also Tronto 1993, 135). Justice considerations are also important in ensuring that the recipients of care are given the proper respect; as Joan Tronto writes, "Without strong conceptions of rights, caregivers are apt to see the world only from their own perspective and to stifle diversity and otherness" (Tronto 1993, 161). Likewise, while an ethic of justice is devoted to equal rights, care considerations seem necessary to develop a morally adequate account of rights. As Narayan writes,

> improvements along care dimensions, such as attentiveness to and concern for human needs and human suffering, might provide the "enabling conditions" for more adequate forms of justice. For instance, attention to the needs, predicaments and suffering of the impoverished and destitute in affluent western societies might result in social policies that institutionalize welfare rights, rights to adequate medical care, and so forth." (Narayan 1995, 139)

Thus the ethic of care and the ethic of justice are interdependent in that each of the ethics provides conditions necessary to a morally adequate version of the other ethic.

Next I will turn to the question of how similar or different the ideal versions of the ethic of care and the ethic of justice are. Two main answers to this question have been offered. One is that care and justice converge into a single comprehensive ethic, and the second is that the two ethics remain independent alternatives. The first view begins with the recognition that each of the two ethics comes in better and worse versions, and that while the worse versions of the ethics are dichotomous, the better versions are not. It concludes that at their best, the two ethics are the same. To assess this view it is important to clarify exactly what is meant by the claim that the two ethics converge, or are the same. They could be the same in every sense, by adopting the same method, the same ontology, the same priorities, and thus reaching the same conclusions, or they could be the same only in the sense that they reach the same or compatible conclusions. Carol Gilligan seems to endorse the minimal sense of convergence in *In a Different Voice*, when she holds that in their most developed forms, the ethic of justice and the ethic of care "converge in the realization that just as inequality adversely affects both parties in an unequal relationship, so too violence is destructive for everyone involved" (Gilligan 1982, 174). That is, the two ethics converge in a *realization*, but they do not converge into a single *ethic*. I think that Gilligan is correct that the ethic of care and the ethic of justice often converge in this minimal sense.

However, this minimal sense of convergence has often been confused with a complete sense of convergence, which lacks comparable support. For the convergence thesis to give a full account of the relationship between the two ethics, it would have to hold that the two ethics converge in every sense. I have challenged the standard accounts of the two ethics as having dichotomous methods, ontologies, and priorities. However, I believe it is a mistake to understand the ethics as converging into a single ethic. Even in their ideal versions, the two ethics draw our attention to different dimensions of any given situation—the ethic of justice to hierarchies among individuals, the ethic of care to the sense of connection among individuals. As I have shown, these different dimensions are related to one another in ways that are often overlooked; for instance, an individual can achieve personal autonomy only by being nurtured by others. However, these dimensions remain distinct; neither ethic can be reduced to the other.

Those who have pursued the convergence approach have typically done so from a justice perspective, arguing that the ethic of care can be assimilated to the ethic of justice. They have argued that what seems to be distinctive of the ethic of care can be translated into the language of the ethic of justice. However, this assimilation is accomplished only by distorting the ethic of care. For instance, it has been argued that care is included in the ethic of justice under the general heading of benevolence. However, benevolence is directed toward people *in general*, while care is directed toward persons *in particular*, so care is not properly understood as benevolence. Joy Kroeger-Mappes has also argued that the attempt to understand care in terms of rights or obligations is an example of such flawed assimilation, as doing so misrepresents the ethic of care by suggesting that a sense of duty is an adequate motive. While I have disagreed with this argument in part, arguing that the ethic of care can (and should) include rights and obligations, I agree that any attempt to fit the care into *traditional* obligation theory distorts care. Thus the view that the ethic of care and the ethic of justice converge into a single ethic theoretically overstates the similarities between the two ethics and in practice tends to distort the distinctive features of the ethic of care.

Another view that feminists have taken on the relationship between care and justice is that the two ethics provide alternative and independent orientations on any given situation, just as a single figure can be seen alternatively as a rabbit or a duck. Here the emphasis is not on the ethics' similarities to one another, but on their differences from one another. As Sara Ruddick writes, "The two moral orientations foster distinctive cognitive capacities, appeal to distinctive ideals of rationality, elicit distinctive moral emotions, presume distinctive conceptions of identity and relationships, recognize distinctive virtues and make distinctive requirements on institutions" (Ruddick 1995, 262). Ruddick holds that because both ethics can be applied to any moral situation, the ethics can check and inform each other. However, "there is no third, 'mature,' single integrative moral perspective within which each orientation has its place" (Ruddick 1995, 262). Thus, according to this approach, moral thinking involves a dialogue between two irreducibly different perspectives, but one which cannot yield a third, comprehensive perspective.

The view that the two ethics provide alternative gestalts on any given situation works better than the convergence view. Most importantly, by insisting that the two ethics represent alternative orientations, this approach refuses to allow the ethic of care to be assimilated into the ethic of justice. However, there is one important disanalogy between the rabbit/duck gestalts and the justice/care gestalts. There is no necessary connection between the rabbit and the duck orientations; that is, a picture of a rabbit need not contain a hidden picture of a duck. However, there is a mutual interdependence between the justice and care orientations. As Alison Jaggar writes, "It is no more than a contingent fact that the outline of the duck can also be seen as the shape of a rabbit and *vice versa*, whereas it is not contingent that particular situations gain their meaning from social structures and that social structures exist only through their instantiation in particular situations" (Jaggar 1995, 20). Jaggar focuses on the interdependence of the abstract and contextual emphases of the two ethics, but, as I have shown, justice and care are interdependent in a number of ways.

The interdependence of justice and care suggests that, contrary to the gestalt view, it may be possible to do more than simply shift back and forth between these two orientations. That is, unlike the relationship between the rabbit and the duck, the relationship between justice and care may itself be informative. In fact, as I showed in Chapter 2, the interaction between justice and care leads us to understand autonomy in a way that neither ethic would understand it alone. Thus there are ways in which the interaction of the two ethics can yield insights that neither ethic would yield on its own. This does not necessarily contradict Ruddick's claim that there is no third ethic which integrates the first two. Focusing on ways in which the ethic of care and the ethic of justice are interrelated would yield an entirely new ethic, with its own ontology, method, and priorities, only if these interrelations pointed to a more basic dimension of human relationships which incorporates, without compromising, all of the features of the first two. If such an ethic exists, no one has found it yet, and it seems highly unlikely that it would exist. But we have seen that the interaction of the two ethics can reveal things that would not be evident by focusing on either the ethic of justice or the ethic of care in isolation from the other.

Thus the convergence view focuses on the interaction between the ethics so much that it conceals the distinctiveness of the ethics, while the gestalt view focuses on the ethics' distinctiveness so much that it conceals (some of) the ways in which the ethics can interact with one another. The fact that the ethic of care and the ethic of justice are interdependent and distinct ethics suggests that we need a third alternative account of their relationship to one another. I think it is helpful to think of care and justice as distinct ethics which can be *integrated* in the sense that they can jointly determine deliberation in public as well as personal contexts. By integrating them in that we use both ethics instead of merely one in any given situation, we acknowledge their interdependence and their distinctiveness.

The two ethics will tend to have different things to offer in particular moral deliberations. For instance, in the Heinz dilemma, the ethic of justice is decisive in telling us that the life of Heinz's wife is worth more than the pharmacist's right to the drug, while the ethic of care helps us figure out the best way to secure the drug, which is not to steal it but to draw upon one's relationships to others. The contributions of the two ethics will not always be consistent with one another. To use an example that Owen Flanagan and Jonathan Adler explore, a university hiring committee may have to weigh the fact that one candidate has already worked for them temporarily and successfully against the fact that an impartial nationwide search would probably point to another candidate (Flanagan and Adler 1983). Integrating the two ethics requires recognizing that such conflicts between the ethic of justice and the ethic of care do not mean that only the ethic of justice is relevant.

Advocates of the ethic of care are often wary of the idea that justice and care should be integrated because of the dangers of assimilation. Just as the well-intentioned "integration" of social groups can in fact be the destruction of a minority culture, there is the danger that, given the traditional prevalence of the ethic of justice, the "integration" of the ethic of justice and the ethic of care will jeopardize the ethic of care's distinctive contributions. Thus it is important to remain aware of our learned tendency to prioritize the ethic of justice and thereby slight the ethic of care whenever the two conflict. Also contributing to this danger is the fact that we want moral problems to have clear-cut answers, and we expect moral theory to provide them for us. This desire to simplify often leads to oversimplification and thus to the trivialization and distortion of the ethic of care. We need to keep in mind that sometimes there will be tensions between different moral concerns that cannot be resolved. In fact, despite the ethic of justice's focus on moral conflicts, justice considerations alone often conflict, such as in rights conflicts, and there is often no metaprinciple that allows us to reconcile these conflicts. Attention to the ethic of care adds to our considerations, and thus to the potential conflicts we face. Adequate moral reasoning will not necessarily yield simple answers, but it will consider all relevant considerations, and both the ethic of justice and the ethic of care direct us to relevant considerations.

It has been said that "the world doesn't need another debate on care versus justice" (Deveaux 1995, 118). I agree, and I have tried to avoid another such debate in this book. However, the ethic of care, the ethic of justice, and their relations to one another remain morally important. I have tried to shift the debate from whether the ethic of care or the ethic of justice is superior to how these two orientations can inform one another. In fact, however, taking this priority is in a sense an endorsement of the ethic of care. It is a recognition that the ethic of care need not defeat the ethic of justice to make its point. Insofar as progress in moral theory results from attention to the relationship between the two ethics rather than from establishing the correct priority of the ethics, the ethic of care will have demonstrated its importance.

Notes

1. I do not think this is Kroeger-Mappes's conclusion, although it is not entirely clear to me what her conclusion is.

Bibliography

Abel, Emily K. and Margaret K. Nelson, eds. 1990. *Circles of Care: Work and Identity in Women's Lives*. Albany: State University of New York Press.

Auerbach, J., et al. 1985. On Gilligan's *In a Different Voice. Feminist Studies* 11 (Spring): 149–61.

Baier, Annette. 1985. What Do Women Want in a Moral Theory? *Nous* 19: 53–63.(Also: 1993. In *An Ethic of Care*, ed. Larrabee, 19–32. New York: Routledge.

Baier, Annette. 1986. Trust and Antitrust. *Ethics* 96 (January): 231–260.

Baier, Annette. 1987a. Hume: The Women's Moral Theorist? In *Women and Moral Theory*, ed. Kittay and Meyers, 37–55. Totowa, NJ: Rowman & Littlefield.

Baier, Annette. 1987b. The Need for More than Justice. In *Science, Morality and Feminist Theory*, ed. Marsha Hanen and Kai Nielsen, 41–56. Calgary, Alberta: The University of Calgary Press.

Baier, Annette. 1995. A Note on Justice, Care, and Immigration Policy. *Hypatia* 10 (Spring): 150–152.

Bane, M. J. 1983. Is the Welfare State Replacing the Family? *Public Interest* 70: 91–101.

Barcalow, Emmett. 1994. *Moral Philosophy: Theories and Issues*. Belmont, CA: Wadsworth Publishing Company.

Bartky, Sandra Lee. 1990. *Femininity and Domination*. New York: Routledge.

Bell, Linda A. 1993. *Rethinking Ethics in the Midst of Violence: A Feminist Approach to Freedom*. Lanham, MD: Rowman & Littlefield.

Benhabib, Seyla. 1987. The Generalized and the Concrete Other. In *Women and Moral Theory*, ed. Kittay and Meyers, 154–177. Totowa, NJ: Rowman & Littlefield.

Benhabib, Seyla. 1992. *Situating the Self*. New York: Routledge.

Benjamin, Martin and Joy Curtis. 1987. Ethical Autonomy in Nursing. In *Health Care Ethics: An Introduction*, ed. Donald VanDeVeer and Tom Regan, 394–427. Philadelphia: Temple University Press.

Blum, Lawrence. 1988. Gilligan and Kohlberg: Implications for Moral Theory. *Ethics* 98 (April): 472–491. (Also: 1993. In *An Ethic of Care*, ed. Larrabee, 49–68. New York: Routledge.)

Blum, Lawrence. 1992. Care. In *Encyclopedia of Ethics*, ed. Becker, 125–127. New York: Garland Publishing, Inc.

Blum, Lawrence, Marcia Homiak, Judy Housman, and Naomi Scheman. 1975. Altruism and Women's Oppression. *Philosophical Forum* 5: 222–247. (Also: 1976. In *Women and Philosophy*, ed. Gould and Wartofsky, 222–247. New York: Putnam.)

Brabeck, Mary, ed. 1989. *Who Cares? Theory, Research, and Educational Implications of the Ethic of Care*. New York: Praeger.

Broughton, John M. 1983. Women's Rationality and Men's Virtues. *Social Research* 50: 597–642. (Also: 1993. In *An Ethic of Care*, ed. Larrabee, 112–142. New York: Routledge.)

Calhoun, Cheshire. 1988. Justice, Care, Gender Bias. *Journal of Philosophy* 85: 451–463.

Cancian, Francesca. 1985. Gender Politics: Love and Power in the Private and Public Spheres. In *Gender and the Life Course*, ed. Alice S. Rossi, 253–264. New York: Aldine Publishing Company.

Cancian, Francesca. 1986. The Feminization of Love. *Signs* 11: 692–709.

Card, Claudia. 1990a. Caring and Evil. *Hypatia* 5 (Spring): 101–108.

Card, Claudia. 1990b. Women's Voices and Ethical Ideals: Must We Mean What We Say? *Ethics* 99 (October): 125–135.

Card, Claudia, ed. 1991. *Feminist Ethics*. Lawrence: University Press of Kansas.

Chodorow, Nancy. 1978. *The Reproduction of Mothering*. Berkeley: University of California Press.

Christman, John, ed. 1989. *The Inner Citadel: Essays on Individual Autonomy*. New York: Oxford University Press.

Code, Lorraine. 1987. Second Persons. In *Science, Morality and Feminist Theory*, ed. Hanen and Nielsen, 357–382. Calgary: University of Calgary Press.

Code, Lorraine, Sheila Mullett, and Christine Overall, eds. 1988. *Feminist Perspectives: Philosophical Essays on Method and Morals*. Toronto: University of Toronto Press.

Cole, Eve Browning and Susan Coultrap-McQuin, eds. 1992. *Explorations in Feminist Ethics*. Bloomington: Indiana University Press.

Collins, Patricia Hill. 1990. *Black Feminist Thought: Knowledge, Consciousness, and the Politics of Empowerment*. Boston: Unwin Hyman.

Cott, Nancy. 1977. *The Bonds of Womanhood*. New Haven: Yale University Press.

Cott, Nancy. 1987. *The Grounding of Modern Feminism*. New Haven: Yale University Press.

Curtin, Deane. 1991. Toward an Ecological Ethic of Care. *Hypatia* 6 (Spring): 60–74.

Daniels, Norman. 1988. *Am I my Parents' Keeper?* New York: Oxford University Press.

Davion, Victoria. 1990. Pacifism and Care. *Hypatia* 5 (Spring): 90–100.

de Beauvoir, Simone. 1952. *The Second Sex*. New York: Vintage.

DeVault, Marjorie. 1991. *Feeding the Family: The Social Organization of Caring as Gendered Work*. Chicago: University of Chicago Press.

Deveaux, Monique. 1995. Shifting Paradigms: Theorizing Care and Justice in Political Theory. *Hypatia* 10 (Spring): 115–119.

Diamond, Irene, ed. 1983. *Families, Politics, and Public Policy*. New York: Longman.

Dietz, Mary. 1985. Citizenship with a Feminist Face. *Political Theory* 13 (February): 19–37.

di Leonardo, Micaela. 1987. The Female World of Cards and Holidays. *Signs* 12: 440–453.

Dillon, Robin. 1992. Care and Respect. In *Explorations in Feminist Ethics*, ed. Cole and Coultrap-McGuin, 69–81. Bloomington: Indiana University Press.

DuBois, Ellen C., Mary C. Dunlap, C. Gilligan, Catherine A. MacKinnon, and Carrie J. Menkel-Meadow, Conversants, with Isabel Marcus and Paul J. Spiegelman, Moderators. 1985. Feminist Discourse, Moral Values and the Law—A Conversation. *Buffalo Law Review* 34: 11–87.

Elshtain, Jean Bethke. 1980. *Public Man, Private Woman*. Princeton: Princeton University Press.

Elshtain, Jean Bethke. 1982. Antigone's Daughters. *Democracy* 2: 46–59.

Elshtain, Jean Bethke and Sheila Tobias, eds. 1990. *Women, Militarism, and War*. Savage, MD: Rowman & Littlefield.

Exdell, John. 1987. Ethics, Ideology, and Feminine Virtue. In *Science, Morality, and Feminism*, ed. Hanen and Nielsen, 169–200. Calgary: University of Calgary Press.

Ezorsky, Gertrude, ed. 1987. *Moral Rights in the Workplace*. Albany: State University of New York Press.

Ferguson, Ann. 1987. A Feminist Aspect Theory of the Self. In *Science, Morality, and Feminist Theory*, ed. Hanen and Nielsen, 339–354. Calgary: University of Calgary Press.

Ferguson, Kathy. 1984. *The Feminist Case against Bureaucracy*. Philadelphia: Temple University Press.

Finch, Janet and Dulcie Groves, eds. 1983. *A Labour of Love: Women, Work and Caring*. London: Routledge and Kegan Paul.

Fisher, Bernice. 1990. Alice in the Human Services. In *Circles of Care*, ed. Abel and Nelson, 108–131. Albany: SUNY Press.

Fisher, Bernice and Joan Tronto. 1990. Toward a Feminist Theory of Caring. In *Circles of Care*, ed. Abel and Nelson, 35–62. Albany: SUNY Press.

Flanagan, Owen. 1982. Virtue, Sex and Gender. *Ethics* 92 (April): 499–512.

Flanagan, Owen and Jonathan Adler. 1983. Impartiality and Particularity. *Social Research* 50: 576–96.

Flanagan, Owen and Kathryn Jackson. 1987. Justice, Care, and Gender: The Kohlberg-Gilligan Debate Revisited. *Ethics* 97 (April): 622–637. (Also: 1993. In *An Ethic of Care*, ed. Larrabee, 69–86. New York: Routledge.)

Fraser, Nancy. 1986. Toward a Discourse Ethic of Solidarity. *Praxis International* 5 (January): 425–429.

Fraser, Nancy. 1993. After the Family Wage: What Do Women Want in Social Welfare? Manuscript.

Frazer, Elizabeth and Nicola Lacey. 1993. *The Politics of Community: A Feminist Critique of the Liberal-Communitarian Debate*. Toronto: University of Toronto Press.

Friedman, Marilyn. 1985. Moral Integrity and the Deferential Wife. *Philosophical Studies* 47: 141–150.

Friedman, Marilyn. 1986. Autonomy and the Split-Level Self. *The Southern Journal of Philosophy* XXIV: 19–35.

Friedman, Marilyn. 1987a. Beyond Caring: The De-Moralization of Gender. In *Science, Morality and Feminist Theory*, ed. Marsha Hanen and Kai Nielsen, 87–110. Calgary: The University of Calgary Press. (Also 1993. In *An Ethic of Care*, ed. Larrabee, 258–274. New York: Routledge.)

Friedman, Marilyn. 1987b. Care and Context in Moral Reasoning. In *Women and Moral Theory*, ed. Kittay and Meyers, 190–204. Totowa, N.J.: Rowman & Littlefield.

Friedman, Marilyn. 1991. The Social Self and the Partiality Debates. In *Feminist Ethics*, ed. Card, 161–179. Lawrence: University Press of Kansas.

Frye, Marilyn. 1983. *The Politics of Reality: Essays in Feminist Theory*. Trumansburg, NY: The Crossing Press.

Gilligan, Carol. 1982. *In a Different Voice: Psychological Theory and Women's Development*. Cambridge, MA: Harvard University Press.

Gilligan, Carol. 1986a. In a Different Voice: Women's Conceptions of Self and of Morality. In *Women and Values*, ed. Pearsall, 309–339. Belmont, CA: Wadsworth Publishing Company.

Gilligan, Carol. 1986b. Remapping the Moral Domain: New Images of the Self in Relationship. In *Reconstructing Individualism: Autonomy, Individuality and the Self in Western Thought*, ed. Heller et al., 237–250. Stanford: Stanford University Press.

Gilligan, Carol. 1986c. Reply. *Signs* 11: 324–33. (Also: 1993. In *An Ethic of Care*, ed. Larrabee, 207–214. New York: Routledge.)

Gilligan, Carol. 1987. Moral Orientation and Moral Development. In *Women and Moral Theory*, ed. Kittay and Meyers, 19–33. Totowa, NJ: Rowman & Littlefield.

Gilligan, Carol and G. Wiggins. 1987. The Origins of Morality in Early Childhood Relationships. In *The Emergence of Mortality in Young Children*, ed. Kagan and Lamb, 277–306.

Gilligan, Carol. 1995. Hearing the Difference: Theorizing Connection. *Hypatia* 10 (Spring): 120–127.

Goodin, Robert. 1985. *Protecting the Vulnerable*. Chicago: The University of Chicago Press.

Goodin, Robert. 1988. *Reasons for Welfare*. Princeton: Princeton University Press.

Graham, Hilary. 1983. Caring: A Labour of Love. In *A Labour of Love: Women, Work and Caring*, ed. Finch and Groves, 13–30. London: Routledge and Kegan Paul.

Greeno, Catherine and Eleanor Maccoby. 1986. How Different is the "Different Voice"? *Signs* 11: 310–316. (Also: 1993. In *An Ethic of Care*, ed. Larrabee, 193–198. New York: Routledge.)

Grimshaw, Jean. 1986. *Philosophy and Feminist Thinking*. Minneapolis: University of Minnesota Press.

Hanen, Marsha, and Kai Nielsen, eds. 1987. *Science, Morality and Feminist Theory*. Calgary: University of Calgary Press.

Harding, Sandra. 1987. The Curious Coincidence of Feminine and African Moralities. In *Women and Moral Theory*, ed. Kittay and Meyers, 296–316. Totowa, NJ: Rowman & Littlefield.

Hartmann, Heidi. 1981. The Family as the Locus of Gender, Class, and Political Struggle: The Example of Housework, *Signs* 6 (Spring): 366–394.

Held, Virginia. 1987a. Feminism and Moral Theory. In *Women and Moral Theory*, ed. Kittay and Meyers, 111–128. Totowa, NJ: Rowman & Littlefield.

Held, Virginia. 1987b. Non-contractual Society. In *Science, Morality and Feminist Theory*, ed. Hanen and Nielsen, 111–138. Calgary: University of Calgary Press.

Held, Virginia. 1993. *Feminist Morality: Transforming Culture, Society, and Politics*. Chicago: The University of Chicago Press.

Held, Virginia, ed. 1995a. *Justice and Care: Essential Readings in Feminist Ethics*. Boulder, CO: Westview Press.

Held, Virginia. 1995b. The Meshing of Care and Justice. *Hypatia* 10 (Spring): 128–132.

Held, Virginia. 1995c. Rights and the Ethic of Care. In *APA Newsletter on Feminism and Philosophy* 94 (Spring): 40–42.

Hill, Thomas. 1973. Servility and Self-Respect. *The Monist* 57: 87–104.

Hill, Thomas. 1987. The Importance of Autonomy. In *Women and Moral Theory*, ed. Kittay and Meyers, 129–138. Totowa, NJ: Rowman & Littlefield.

Hill, Thomas. 1989. The Kantian Conception of Autonomy. In *The Inner Citadel*, ed. Christman, 91–108. Oxford: Oxford University Press.

Hirschmann, Nancy. 1992. *Rethinking Obligation: A Feminist Method for Political Theory.* Ithaca: Cornell University Press.

Hoagland, Sarah Lucia. 1990. Some Concerns about Nel Noddings' Caring. *Hypatia* 5 (Spring): 115–119.

Hochschild, Arlie. 1983. *The Managed Heart.* Berkeley: University of California Press.

Hochschild, Arlie. 1989. *The Second Shift.* New York: Viking Penguin, Inc.

Houston, Barbara. 1987. Rescuing Womanly Virtues. In *Science, Morality and Feminist Theory,* ed. Hanen and Nielsen, 237–262. Calgary: University of Calgary Press.

Houston, Barbara. 1988. Gilligan and the Politics of a Distinctive Women's Morality. In *Feminist Perspectives,* eds. Code, Mullett, and Overall, 168–189. Toronto: University of Toronto Press.

Houston, Barbara. 1989. Prolegomena to Future Caring. In Brabeck, *Who Cares?,* ed. Brabeck, 84–100. New York: Praeger.

Houston, Barbara. 1990. Caring and Exploitation. *Hypatia* 5 (Spring): 115–119.

Imray, Linda and A. Middleton. 1983. Public and Private: Marking the Boundaries. In *The Public and the Private,* ed. Gamarmikov et al., 12–37. London: Heinemann.

Jaggar, Alison. 1991. Feminist Ethics: Projects, Problems, Prospects. In *Feminist Ethics,* ed. Card, 78–104. Lawrence, KA: University Press of Kansas.

Jaggar, Alison. 1994. Introduction: Living with Contradictions. In *Living with Contradictions: Controversies in Feminist Social Ethics,* ed. Jaggar, 1–12. Boulder, CO: Westview Press.

Jaggar, Alison. 1995. Caring as a Feminist Practice of Moral Reason. In *Justice and Care: Essential Readings,* ed. Held, 179-202. Boulder, CO: Westview Press.

Kasachkoff, Tziporah. 1987. Nursing Ethics and Hospital Work. In *Moral Rights in the Workplace,* ed. Ezorsky, 236–248. Albany: SUNY Press.

Keller, Catherine. 1986. *From a Broken Web: Separation, Sexism and Self.* Boston: Beacon Press.

Kerber, Linda, Catherine Green, Eleanor Maccoby, Zella Luria, Carol Stack, and Carol Gilligan. 1986. In A Different Voice: An Interdisciplinary Forum. *Signs* 11: 304–333.

Kittay, Eva, and Diana Meyers, eds. 1987. *Women and Moral Theory.* Totowa, NJ: Rowman & Littlefield.

Kohlberg, Lawrence. 1969. Stage and Sequence: The Cognitive Developmental Approach to Socialization. In D.A. Goslin, ed., *Handbook of Socialization Theory and Research.* Chicago: Rand McNally.

Kohlberg, Lawrence. 1981. *Essays on Moral Development.* Vol. 1: *The Philosophy of Moral Development.* San Francisco: Harper & Row.

Kohlberg, Lawrence. 1982. A Reply to Owen Flanagan and Some Comments on the Puka-Goodpaster Exchange. *Ethics* 92: 513–528.

Kohlberg, Lawrence. 1984. *Essays on Moral Development.* Vol. 2: *The Psychology of Moral Development.* New York: Harper & Row.

Kohlberg, Lawrence, with Charles Levine and Alexandra Hewer. 1984. The Current Formulation of the Theory. In *The Psychology of Moral Development: The Nature and Validity of Moral Stages.* New York: Harper & Row.

Kroeger-Mappes, Joy. 1991. Ethical Dilemmas for Nurses: Physician's Orders versus Patient's Rights. In *Biomedical Ethics,* ed. Mappes and Zembaty, 150–156. New York: McGraw-Hill, Inc.

Kroeger-Mappes, Joy. 1994. The Ethic of Care vis-a-vis the Ethic of Rights: A Problem for Contemporary Moral Theory. *Hypatia* 9 (Summer): 108–131.

Land, Hilary. 1978. Who Cares for the Family? *Journal of Social Policy* 7 (July): 257–284.

Larrabee, Mary Jeanne, ed. 1993. *An Ethic of Care: Feminist and Interdisciplinary Perspectives.* New York: Routledge.

Levine, Helen. 1982. The Personal is Political: Feminism and the Helping Professions. In *Feminism in Canada*, ed. Miles and Finn, 175–210. Montreal: Black Rose Books.

Manning, Rita. 1992. *Speaking from the Heart: A Feminist Perspective on Ethics.* Lanham, MD: Rowman & Littlefield.

Mansbridge, Jane. 1991a. Feminism and Democracy. In *The American Prospect* 1 (Spring): 126–139.

Mansbridge, Jane. 1991b. "Difference" as a Feminist Political Strategy. Manuscript.

McDowell, Linda and Pringle, eds. 1992. *Defining Women: Social Institutions and Gender Divisions.* Cambridge, England: Polity Press.

Meyers, Diana. 1987a. Personal Autonomy and the Paradox of Feminine Socialization. *Journal of Philosophy* 84 (November): 619–629.

Meyers, Diana. 1987b. The Socialized Individual and Individual Autonomy. In *Women and Moral Theory*, ed. Kittay and Meyers, 139–153. Totowa, NJ: Rowman & Littlefield.

Meyers, Diana. 1989. *Self, Society and Personal Choice.* New York: Columbia University Press.

Minow, Martha. 1991. *Making All the Difference.* Cambridge: Harvard University Press.

Moody-Adams, Michele M. 1991. Gender and the Complexity of Moral Voices. In *Feminist Ethics*, ed. Claudia Card, 195–212. Lawrence, KA: University Press of Kansas.

Morgan, Kathryn. 1987. Women and Moral Madness. In *Science, Morality and Feminist Theory*, ed. Hanen and Nielsen, 201–226. Calgary: The University of Calgary Press.

Mullett, Sheila. 1988. Shifting Perspectives: A New Approach to Ethics. In *Feminist Perspectives*, ed. Code, Mullett, and Overall, 109–126. Toronto: University of Toronto Press.

Narayan, Uma. 1995. Colonialism and Its Others: Considerations on Rights and Care Discourses. *Hypatia* 10 (Spring): 133–140.

Nedelsky, Jennifer. 1989. Reconceiving Autonomy: Sources, Thoughts and Possibilities. *Yale Journal of Law and Feminism* 1: 7–36.

Newton, Lisa. 1981. In Defense of the Traditional Nurse. *Nursing Outlook* 29: 348–354.

Nicholson, Linda. 1983a. Feminist Theory: the Private and the Public. In *Beyond Domination*, ed. Gould, 221–233. Totowa, NJ: Rowman & Allanheld.

Nicholson, Linda. 1983b. Women, Morality and History. *Social Research* 50: 514–536, (Also: 1993. In *An Ethic of Care*, ed. Larrabee, 87–101. New York: Routledge.)

Nicholson, Linda. 1986. *Gender and History.* New York: Columbia University Press.

Nielsen, Kai. 1987. Afterward. In *Science, Morality and Feminist Theory*, ed. Hanen and Nielsen, 383–418. Calgary: University of Calgary Press.

Noddings, Nel. 1984. *Caring: A Feminine Approach to Ethics and Moral Education.* Berkeley: University of California Press.

Noddings, Nel. 1990a. Ethics from the Standpoint of Women. In *Theoretical Perspectives on Sexual Difference*, ed. Deborah Rhode, 160–173. New Haven: Yale University Press.

Noddings, Nel. 1990b. A Response. *Hypatia* 5 (Spring): 120–126.

Noddings, Nel. 1991. The Alleged Parochialism of Caring. In *APA Newsletter on Feminism and Philosophy* 90 (Winter): 96–98.

Nunner-Winkler, Gertrud. 1993. Two Moralities? In *An Ethic of Care*, ed. Larrabee, 143–156. New York: Routledge.

Okin, Susan Moller. 1989a. *Justice, Gender, and the Family.* New York: Basic Books.

Okin, Susan Moller. 1989b. Reason and Feeling in Thinking about Justice. *Ethics* 99: 229–249.

Okin, Susan Moller. 1990. Thinking like a Woman. In *Theoretical Perspectives on Sexual Difference*, ed. Rhode, 145–159. New Haven: Yale University Press.

Okin, Susan Moller. 1991. Gender, the Public and the Private. In *Political Theory Today*, ed. Held, 68–90. Stanford: Stanford University Press.

O'Neill, Onora. 1992. Charity. In *Encyclopedia of Ethics*, ed. Becker, 134–136. New York: Garland Publishing, Inc.

Pateman, Carol. 1987. Feminist Critiques of the Public/Private Dichotomy. In *Feminism and Equality*, ed. Anne Phillips, 103–126. Oxford: Basil Blackwell.

Pateman, Carol. 1988. *The Sexual Contract*. Stanford: Stanford University Press.

Pearsall, Marilyn, ed. 1986. *Women and Values: Readings in Recent Feminist Philosophy*. Belmont, CA: Wadsworth Publishing Company.

Pollitt, Katha. 1992. Are Women Morally Superior to Men? *The Nation* : 12/28/92, 799–807.

Pringle, Rosemary. 1992. Women and Consumer Capitalism. In *Defining Women*, ed. McDowell and Pringle, 148–152. Cambridge, England: Polity Press.

Puka, Bill. 1990. The Liberation of Caring: A Different Voice for Gilligan's "Different Voice." *Hypatia* 5 (Spring): 58–82. (Also: 1993. In *An Ethic of Care*, ed. Larrabee, 215–239. New York: Routledge.)

Reverby, Susan. 1990. The Duty or Right to Care? In *Circles of Care*, ed. Abel and Nelson, 132–149. Albany: SUNY Press.

Romain, Diane. 1992. Care and Confusion. In *Explorations in Feminist Ethics*, ed. Cole and Coultrap-McQuin, 27–37. Bloomington: Indiana University Press.

Rooney, Phyllis. 1991. A Different Different Voice. *The Philosophical Forum* XXII: 335–361.

Rose, Hilary. 1986. Women's Work: Women's Knowledge. In *What is Feminism?* ed. Mitchell and Oakley, 161–183. New York: Pantheon Books.

Ruddick, Sara. 1983a. Maternal Thinking. In *Mothering*, ed. Trebilcot, 213–230. Totowa, NJ: Rowman and Allenheld.

Ruddick, Sara. 1983b. Preservative Love and Military Destruction. In *Mothering*, ed. Trebilcot, 231–262. Totowa, NJ: Rowman and Allanheld.

Ruddick, Sara. 1989. *Maternal Thinking: Toward a Politics of Peace*. Boston: Beacon Press.

Ruddick, Sara. 1992. War and Peace. In *Encyclopedia of Ethics*, ed. Becker, 1297–1304. New York: Garland Publishing Company.

Ruddick, Sara. 1995. Injustice in Families: Assault and Domination. In *Justice and Care: Essential Readings*, ed Held, 203–223. Boulder, CO: Westview Press.

Sacks, Karen Brodkin. 1990. Does It Pay to Care? In *Circles of Care*, ed. Abel and Nelson, 188–206. Albany: SUNY Press.

Sandel, Michael. 1982. *Liberalism and the Limits of Justice*. Cambridge: Cambridge University Press.

Scheman, Naomi. 1983. Individualism and the Objects of Psychology. In *Discovering Reality*, ed. Sandra Harding and Merrill B. Hintikka, 225–244. Boston: D. Reidel Publishing Company.

Schwartz, Adina. 1982. Meaningful Work. *Ethics* 92: 634–646.

Schwartz, Adina. 1984. Autonomy in the Workplace. In *Just Business*, ed. Regan, 129–166. New York: Random House.

Scott, Joan. 1988. Deconstructing Equality-Versus-Difference. In *Feminist Studies* 14 (Spring): 33–50.

Sher, George. 1987. Other Voices, Other Rooms? Women's Psychology and Moral Theory. In *Women and Moral Theory*, ed. Kittay and Meyers, 178–189. Totowa, NJ: Rowman & Littlefield.

Singer, Peter. 1972. Famine, Affluence and Morality. *Philosophy and Public Affairs* 1 (Spring): 229–243.

Singer, Peter. 1979. *Practical Ethics.* Cambridge: Cambridge University Press.

Spelman, Elizabeth V. 1991. The Virtue of Feeling and the Feeling of Virtue. In *Feminist Ethics,* ed. Card, 213–232. Lawrence: University Press of Kansas.

Stacey, Judith. 1983. The New Conservative Feminism. *Feminist Studies* 9 (Fall): 559–583.

Stacey, Judith. 1986. Are Feminists Afraid to Leave Home? In *What is Feminism?* ed. Mitchell and Oakley, 208–237. New York: Pantheon Books.

Stocker, Michael. 1987. Duty and Friendship. In *Women and Moral Theory,* ed. Kittay and Meyers, 56–68. Totowa, NJ: Rowman & Littlefield.

Strickling, Bonnelle Lewis. 1988. Self-Abnegation. In *Feminist Perspectives,* ed. Code, Mullett, and Overall, 190–202. Toronto: University of Toronto Press.

Tong, Rosemarie. 1993. *Feminine and Feminist Ethics.* Belmont, CA: Wadsworth Publishing Company.

Tronto, Joan. 1987. Beyond Gender Difference to a Theory of Care. *Signs* 12 : 644–63. (Also: 1993. In *An Ethic of Care,* ed. Larrabee, 240–257. New York: Routledge.)

Tronto, Joan. 1993. *Moral Boundaries: A Political Argument for an Ethic of Care.* New York: Routledge.

Tronto, Joan. 1995. Care as a Basis for Radical Political Judgments. *Hypatia* 10 (Spring): 141–149.

Ungerson, Clare. 1983a. Why Do Women Care? In *A Labour of Love,* ed. Finch and Groves, 31–49. London: Routledge and Kegan Paul.

Ungerson, Clare. 1983b. Women and Caring: Skills, Tasks, and Taboos. In *The Public and the Private,* ed. Gamarmikov et al., 66–77. London: Heinemann.

Veatch, R. M. 1972. Medical Ethics: professional or universal? *Harvard Theological Review* 65: 531–559.

Waerness, Kari. 1984a. Caring as Women's Work in the Welfare State. In *Patriarchy in a Welfare Society,* ed. Holter, 67–87. Oslo: Universitetsforlaget.

Waerness, Kari. 1984b. The Rationality of Caring. *Economic and Industrial Democracy* 5: 185–211.

Walzer, Michael. 1977. *Just and Unjust Wars.* New York: Basic Books.

Williams, Bernard. 1981. *Moral Luck.* Cambridge: Cambridge University Press.

Williams, Joan. 1989. Deconstructing Gender. *Michigan Law Review* 87: 797–845. (Also: 1991. In *Feminist Legal Theory,* ed. Bartlett and Kennedy, 95–123. Boulder, CO: Westview Press.)

Wolfe, Alan. 1989. *Whose Keeper? Social Science and Moral Obligation.* Berkeley: University of California Press.

Young, Iris Marion. 1985. Humanism, Gynocentricism, and Feminist Politics. *Women's Studies International Forum* (Hypatia) 8, no. 3 (1985): 173–183.

Young, Iris Marion. 1990. *Throwing Like a Girl and Other Essays in Feminist Philosophy and Social Theory.* Bloomington: Indiana University Press.

About the Book and Author

Newcomers and more experienced feminist theorists will welcome this even-handed survey of the care/justice debate within feminist ethics. Grace Clement clarifies the key terms, examines the arguments and assumptions of all sides to the debate, and explores the broader implications for both practical and applied ethics. Readers will appreciate her generous treatment of the feminine, feminist, and justice-based perspectives that have dominated the debate.

Clement also goes well beyond description and criticism, advancing the discussion through the incorporation of a broad range of insights into a new integration of the values of care and justice.

Care, Autonomy, and Justice marks a major step forward in our understanding of feminist ethics. It is both direct and helpful enough to work as an introduction for students and insightful and original enough to make it necessary reading for scholars.

Grace Clement is assistant professor of philosophy at Salisbury State University.

Index

Abel, Emily, 47–48, 62
Abortion, 36, 102
Absolute pacifism, 96–97
Abstract/concrete dichotomy, 5, 11, 19,
    89, 112, 118, 120
  conventional boundaries and, 76–80
  Heinz dilemma and, 12–13, 77–78, 79,
    80
  maternal pacifism and, 93–95
Abstract formalism, 78–79
Abstraction, 111. *See also* Abstract/concrete
  dichotomy
Abusive relationships, 38, 72
Adler, Jonathan, 121
Aristotelians, 4, 14
Arrogant eye, 30, 31
Auerbach, J., 40
Autonomy, 7, 8, 13, 15–16, 21–44,
    45–65
  critical thought in, 25–26, 29, 37–38,
    46, 47, 63
  defined, 22–27
  elder-care and, 100–101, 102
  impediments to, 22–23
  individualistic approach to, 26, 27–35,
    43
  institutional conflicts between care and,
    56–65
  interaction between care and justice in,
    120
  in Kantian theory, 4
  as self-determination, 15, 22, 26, 110

social approach to. *See* Social approach
symbolic conflicts between care and,
  49–56

Baier, Annette, 31, 71
Barcalow, Emmett, 13
Benevolence, 119
Benhabib, Seyla, 12, 115
Benjamin, Martin, 47, 63, 64
Blum, Lawrence, 27, 28, 29, 30, 32, 38, 40
Broughton, John, 17, 19

Calhoun, Cheshire, 5, 110, 112
Cancian, Francesca, 52, 53
Card, Claudia, 17
Care. *See also* Distorted care; Genuine care;
  Ideal Type of care
  autonomy compatibility with, 21–44
  conventional boundaries of. *See*
    Conventional boundaries
  femininity of, 49–52
  individualistic approach to, 26, 27–35,
    43
  institutional conflicts between autonomy
    and, 56–65
  integrating justice with, 114–122
  parochial ethic of, 68–69
  personal ethic of, 68–69
  personal service distinguished from,
    47–48
  public applications of. *See* Maternal paci-
    fism; Welfare programs

▼